Miracles in the Mundane

Miracles in the Mundane

Vicki Easterly

ISBN-13: 9781979498005
ISBN-10: 1979498008

Contents

Introduction · · · 1
The Move · · · 7
Miracles Through the Year · · · 15
Kids · · · 61
Grand Kids · · · 83
With Love Comes the Mourning · · · 103
Everyday Miracle People · · · 119
Facebook Stories · · · 157
Miscellaneous Miracles · · · 173

There are only two ways to live your life:
As though nothing is a miracle, or as though everything is a miracle.

Albert Einstein

Introduction

The Prompting

On December 28, 2014, Corky Herbert, a fellow Stephen minister, shared a story of how God had blessed her that day. It was not a parting of the seas miracle, but a gentle whisper to her from God, and how she was able to bless another soul. Through Corky, God prompted me to begin this book.

As I was contemplating whether to begin, the prompting grew louder, so I sought guidance in the Bible. I was led to Luke 9:62. Jesus said, "No procrastination; no backward looks. You can't put off God's kingdom till tomorrow. Seize the day!" So, with that unequivocal message, I gave life to this compilation.

Still, it has taken me three years. Thanks to those of you who shared your stories, and to you storytellers unaware, whose stories I have included. This is a book of "God experiences," of miracles great and small. Now enjoy the blessings of others, and may you be blessed in the reading.

People You Will Meet Here

Welcome! Come on in. The coffee's on. I'll tell you some thoughts that have come to me over this steaming mug. Some are miracles in the mundane, some are simple reflections. Some are about beauty and nature, trees and flowers, stained glass and shiny earrings, and illness and wellness. Some will give you goose-bumps; some will give you smiles. Some will give you pause.

But first, let me introduce you to the people you will meet in this book. I'll start with the people I love the most. I guess we all love our families most. You'll meet my daddy, Russell; my mother, Ann; and my sister, Debbie. My son, Chad, is 46 and the warrior/protector/father of the family. Jen is his sweet, quiet wife. My son, Chris, is 42 and the writer/producer/filmmaker. He is also my editor.

Debbie's girls, Jo and Dale, came next. Jo is a gorgeous 39-year-old blonde real estate agent; Dale is a stunning 32-year-old redheaded nurse. Where did the time go? Now I have the most beautiful dark-haired, brown-eyed granddaughters. Sophie is almost 13; Makayla is five. They are my reward for raising two rambunctious boys. Susie and Teresa are my fun cousins. Teresa is married to John.

I tend to keep my friends for the longest time. Ellie has been my soul friend since 1975, when we met at work, shortly after graduating college. Cathy and I have spun around together in our ADHD world since we shared an office space, when I opened my business in 1994. Martha is my sweet friend, who prayed me through some of my darkest days. Camille, Judy, and Carolyn have been my lunch buddies. Claudette, Betty, and Debra are my Bible study buddies, Scrabble partners, and writer's club encouragers. Elsie is the godmother of my heart.

My life the past seven years has been so enriched by the members of First United Methodist Church in Frankfort, Kentucky. I just live around the corner, so I walk there to the stone church with the stained glass windows, built in 1858. Dr. Phil is our beloved Teddy bear pastor. When you hear me tell about these folks, you will know they are from church: Cleland, Joanie, Ann, Jean, Sarah, and Corky are my fellow Stephen ministers. Judie, Patsy, Sally, Rosie, Margaret, and Jimmie are mentioned too. There are so many other wonderful church people, but I only included these characters this time. I'll tell you about some more the next time. There are people I knew for only a few short days on my Emmaus walk—people like Charlene, and Elaine, and Rachel, who nevertheless, made an impression on me.

I will tell you about miracle people, some of whom are no longer on this earth. Tom was my husband for a very short while, much too short. I'll tell you stories about Aunt Jessie, Grandma Easterly, my baby brother, Miss Vivien C. Moore, Ashley, Halcyon, Robert, Eva, Jimmy, Dr. Scaff, Johnnie, the soldier, and Shannon. Most importantly, I hope you will meet Jesus face-to-face in these stories. I have chosen to capitalize His name each time I have mentioned Him, to give Him all the glory.

It's true, though, that we all have dark-souled people, who creep into our lives. Although it is difficult, I will tell you about the man I married after Tom died, whose name I refuse to utter. And my brother-in-law, whose name I have changed to protect the guilty. These people I mention only to share that miracles can come out of evil. With the passing of time, I can say I would offer even them a cup of cold water if they were thirsty (Mark 9:41). It's about the miracle of forgiveness. Some names I have changed to protect the innocent and downtrodden, as well as the not-so-innocent, but trying-to-do better.

Jennifer was the first person to share her blessing story with me. Sara, Debbie, Kari, Kathy, Sherrel, Ellen, Peggy, Jeannie, Doug, Janna, and Heather shared their own thoughts, as well. I want to be sure they get credit for their contributions.

This book would not have come about without all the people I have introduced you to just now—the good, the bad, the rich, the poor, the beautiful, the average, the sick, the healthy, the young, the old, the dead, the alive. Because people are what it's all about. That's why we call it life. And life is full of miracles in the mundane.

I have also included several blank pages in the back of the book where you can record your own miracles.

Anyway, pull up a chair. Do you want cream and sugar? Have a cherry pastry. Just sit with me and enjoy God's beautiful world. So, where to begin. Let's see, I think I'll start with…

The Move

Good Writing Weather

...To enjoy your work and accept your lot in life—This is indeed a gift from God. God keeps such people so busy enjoying life that they take no time to brood over the past.

Ecclesiastes 5:19-20 NLT

The April temperatures had been in the eighties, much too beautiful to stay indoors. Yesterday, the sweet-smelling lilac enticed me outdoors, where I reveled in the sight of the bright red and yellow tulips and feathery maroon columbine. The redbuds budded and the tree leaves greened, but I needed to write. I needed a day of cold, rainy, gloomy weather.

I realize not many people request a gloomy day, but such a day is so conducive to writing. The forecast said today would be the day. Sure enough, I awoke before dawn to dark, brooding clouds. Rain gently drenched my petunias, as if lulling them into a deep sleep. When I opened the door, I was greeted by the chilly 53-degree air. Perfect!

By eight o'clock, I was at my computer, my Bible, coffee, pen and paper at hand. I typed all day, editing, and searching for scripture to accompany my stories. One story piled on top of another. It was three o'clock when I closed my computer and quit for the day. And it was three o'clock when the sun came shining through, as if to smile on the work I had accomplished today!

My Trees

For I am like the olive tree, thriving in the house of God. I will always trust in God's unfailing love. I will praise you forever, O God, for what you have done.

Psalm 52:8 NIV

The giant sycamore tree across the street from my front window provided the first hints of each changing season. For four years, 16 seasons, I watched that tree from the living room of my rented apartment. In January, it was black, gnarled, and barren. Tiny neon buds heralded in the spring, yielding to a verdant dressing in summer. Autumn was my favorite, with its leaves bursting into vivid colors of sienna, orange, red, and gold. I enjoyed it most the Fall of 2015. I had become familiar with its changing personalities; I considered it "my" tree, and I expectantly awaited the next seasonal display. But it was not to be. When the tree was naked in January 2016, my landlord informed me he was moving his law office into my apartment.

After a hurried and prayerful search, I found another apartment in sight of our beautiful capitol building, which is lined with trees. By the end of January, I was looking out the window at the dark, arthritic tree in the median, comforted by the yellow glow of the decorative street lights, feeling slightly unsettled, not quite at home yet, stuck inside by a raging blizzard; yet assured that my new tree would soon excite my heart with its bright pubescent buds, then dress for me in its lush coat of green, followed by a fashion show of splendid color. Not the same old tree, just a different tree, and I eagerly awaited the performances. Like a tree, I had been uprooted, but I was home after all.

The Move

Dear brothers and sisters, when troubles of any kind come your way, consider it an opportunity for great joy. For you know that when your faith is tested, your endurance has a chance to grow. So let it grow, for when your endurance is fully developed, you will be perfect and complete, needing nothing.

JAMES 1:2-4 NLT

What a mild winter we had that year! It didn't snow until the weekend of my move. Still, it wasn't icy or frigid. Chad, Jen, Chris, and Debbie helped me pack and move to my new apartment, which had 15 steps up to the front of the building.

I spent the first week in my new place listening to Pandora, while I somewhat haphazardly found a place for my belongings. It was tiring, yet exciting; chaotic, yet hopeful. I did not ask for this move; it was thrust on me. I felt overwhelmed and a little irritated. Being ADHD, I was spinning and a bit disorganized. I stocked my kitchen, but couldn't remember where I put what. Slowly, I began to settle in.

Then it hit—the blizzard of 2016. There is no way we could have moved that weekend. Ice and deep snow covered the treacherous steps. God had looked after us in our move last weekend. Though feeling unsettled, I was indeed settled, not in my dream house with granite countertops, but in a charming older apartment.

I was warm. I had time to leisurely finish putting my canned goods in the cabinets. My mind had quieted enough to remember where I had put the peanut butter. I took a roast from the freezer and put it in the crock pot with potatoes, carrots, and onions. Soon I recognized the aromatic cooking smells—the smells of home! I had food; I had heat; I had a comfortable couch. I settled into it, and in the stillness, God filled my heart with joy and my head with more stories. I had what I needed.

The Curtains

I will praise You, O Lord, with all my heart.

Psalm 138:1 NIV

Along with my recent move came the need for new curtains. I measured carefully, then headed out on my curtain search. I found them at Tuesday Morning—mid-century orange curtains with an embossed geometric pattern. The store had six panels; I needed six panels, so I bought them all. When I got home I found that, per usual, I had mis-measured. (Haven't I mentioned I am ADHD?) Really I needed eight panels, but I had bought all that I could find.

Women who shop at Tuesday Morning know that you get what you get, in the quantity they have, on the day you venture in—that's it. But I had to try. Clutching the SKU number, I returned to the store in one last desperate attempt to get my two panels.

I scoured the store alone. Then I asked a worker if they could get more. She said no. She offered to check the computer to see if the other stores had them. Cincinnati had four, which they refused to ship here. Then my home improvement angel looked again. The computer showed that they *did* have another set.

That worker even offered to help me find them. We walked every aisle, scooting scads of curtains aside, until—at last, buried behind a wall of beige panels, she found my orange curtains! Maybe this was not the richest blessing ever, but I sure needed those curtains, and I sure appreciated her kindness. I love my eight panels of orange curtains, and my day is brighter—and that's a good enough miracle.

Unplugged

For six days, work is to be done, but the seventh day shall be your holy day, a Sabbath of rest to the Lord.

Exodus 35:2 NIV

Just as I was heading out the door for Bible study and church this morning, my son headed in the door. He had decided Sunday morning would be the time he was ready to hang my orange curtains and the pictures in my new apartment. He brought his tools and Kayla.

Now it is impossible to hang curtains with a 3-year-old underfoot, so mimi had to stay and run interference. Kayla emptied the Scrabble letters onto the floor, among the rods and hooks; she wanted Froot Loops, chocolate milk, and a bologna face sandwich. While fixing the bologna face, I heard a distraught call for help. I ran to find she had closed a drawer on her fingers. Ouch! I ran for a cold, wet rag, which heals little fingers nicely.

The pounding of the hammer kept time with the pounding of my developing headache. The TV commentators recited endlessly the results of the Presidential polls. The noise and the cacophony were splintering my nerves. Oh, how I needed quiet!

Then I remembered this was First United Methodist Church's "unplugged" Sunday of silence. Truthfully, I had wondered if I could go all afternoon without using my cell phone, TV, or computer. Now I was actually anticipating the silence.

My helpers left at 11:17 a.m.—too late for church, but just in time to unplug. What a peaceful afternoon it has been. I decided to write devotional stories in my quiet time. I asked God (silently) to put them in my head, so that I could put them on paper with a pen. He gave me four stories—stories I might never have written if I had not been "unplugged."

My Stained Glass

Do not store up for yourselves treasures on earth, where moth and rust destroy, and where thieves break in and steal.

MATTHEW 6:19 NIV

I had a collection of stained glass windows, most in the original chipped wooden frames. I loved my stained glass. I kept them in the deep window sills of my historic home. I delighted every morning as I was greeted with a shining show of colors, reflecting in the morning sun.

I spent hours wondering where my stained glass had come from. I imagined that some had rattled at the mighty gospel songs that rung from a southern black church; others, I told myself, came from 1800's Appalachian Apostolic churches, where spirited music could be heard throughout the hollows if those windows were opened. Still others I pictured came from austere white clapboard Baptist churches, where congregations sang the invitational "Just As I Am," while the crystal lights danced around the room.

Then one day I had to move. My new home had modern, thin windowsills. There was nowhere to display my stained glass. Sadly, I took them to a consignment antique shop, where they quickly sold.

Later, I found another historic house and moved in. Charming, thick windowsills were throughout, but my beautiful stained glass was gone. As I sat down to breakfast the first morning in my new house, I looked out my dining room window. There in the second floor window of the house next door was my old favorite stained glass, wood frame and all! I smile happily each morning now as I sip my first cup of coffee and stare out the window at "my" stained glass.

Miracles Through the Year

Miracle In Flight

If he cries to me, I will hear, for I am compassionate.

Exodus 22:27 NIV

Teresa and John took their February cruise to the Caribbean, as they had for the past 16 years. This year would be special. Teresa and John had survived Teresa's bout with Stage IV cancer. She was now miraculously healed. The first seven days were relaxing and fun.

On day eight, John was a little congested and having some trouble breathing. On day nine, they were scheduled to return home. By now, John was having serious breathing difficulties. When they arrived at the Cincinnati airport, Teresa asked for a wheelchair, but was told there were none available. John could barely walk, so Teresa held him up the best she could, while carrying their bags all the way to Gate 78. With Teresa's help, John made it onto the plane.

Within 10 minutes, he was gasping for air. His nails were turning blue. "Don't you dare die on me on this plane!" Teresa beseeched, as she pushed the emergency button. A flight attendant came immediately. She sent an announcement out, asking if there was a doctor on board.

Two rows back, a man rose from his seat and hurried to John. He quickly determined that John needed oxygen. The plane was equipped with two canisters, each one good for one hour. The flight was to be two hours. John calmed at this news. The doctor stayed with John throughout the flight, and called ahead for medics to be waiting upon landing.

He told Teresa he had lived in North Carolina for 30 years, and had only recently moved to Cincinnati; otherwise he would never have been on this flight. He refused money from John and Teresa, as well as the airline's offer of a free flight for literally saving John's life that day. The doctor's name was Fred Zeller; his specialty: Critical Care Pulmonology.

February 15

But I have this complaint against you. You don't love me or each other as you did at first! Look how far you have fallen! Turn back to me and do the works you did at first.

Revelation 2:4-5 NLT

Here it is February 15, and I'm still fat. February 15, the day we leave for our Florida vacation. February 15, the departure date I have known about for six months. I had the best intentions of going to the gym to slim down and bulk up, but I never did. Instead, I plopped on the couch and ate cookies. Hey, it's been snowy and icy—way too cold to get outside; way too cozy inside.

Why do I tell you this? Because it's the way I put off God, too. I love God, but I'm too comfortable in my little nest of sin, too busy to talk one-on-one with Him, too tired, too fearful of the future if I step out in faith and fearlessly grab his hand.

I'm too ashamed to come clean with him. He already knows. Too this, too that, too full of vacuous excuses, even though I know the day is coming.

So I need to take action now, whether it be a big or small matter between me and my God. No longer will I sit and get fat with apathy, putting God aside. He has given His life's blood for me, and promised me a glorious day of salvation. All I need to do is get ready. Tomorrow, February 16, could be the day.

To Be, Or Not To Be

Be careful not to do your acts of righteousness before men, to be seen. If you do, you will have no reward from your Father in heaven.

Matthew 6:1 NIV

I love my church; I wanted to serve. Because I like people, I decided to be a greeter. To be a greeter requires only that I stand, smile and offer a warm welcome. I e-mailed the volunteer coordinator with my wish to serve, except I absent-mindedly typed "Usher." Then I forgot about the e-mail. The usher-greeter list came out on Valentine's Day. To my horror, I had indeed been placed on the usher list.

But I can't be an usher! I'm too clumsy. What if I drop the plates, or pass the plate down the wrong pew? What if I trip and tumble down the aisle? What if? What if? My rational mind knew it was about serving, it was not about me. Yet in my panic, I had begun to focus on "me." I asked for scripture, hoping for a soothing "You will do fine, my child" verse that would affirm that I should be an usher. Instead, I got the admonishing Matthew 6:1

Being an usher requires one to be before men, but *not* necessarily to be seen. So, I will usher. Maybe I will drop the plate, or fall down, or commit some embarrassing faux pas, but God and my church will forgive that and maybe even get a good laugh at my expense, as long as I serve with humility and a right heart.

Miracle On 385

For by grace you have been saved through faith—and that not from yourselves, it is the gift of God...

Ephesians 2:8 NIV

February 22, 2016, Memphis, Tennessee, from the WMCA Action News 5

A car burst into flames on Highway 385 near the Ridgeway exit ramp. The vehicle went off the road and ran into a pole. The driver was pinned against the steering wheel. "Bystanders started getting stuff to bust the windows," a witness said.

Moments later everyone on the scene heard the car making loud popping noises. "The car is going to blow, Lord. Please let me get this man out!" one man begged, as he pulled the man from the car.

Seconds after the driver was extricated, the car exploded and burned to a hull. The driver was taken to the hospital with critical injuries.

Police recovered one item from the burned-out car—a perfectly intact Bible. "That is God," said a witness named Eugene. "If you don't believe it, I don't know what to say." But we do. We know it was God's amazing, saving grace in action.

Cinderella's Closet

How beautiful you are, my darling! Oh, how beautiful!

Song Of Songs 1:15 NIV

It happens in March, but preparations last all year. How can I describe the miracle that is Cinderella's Closet—a day of pure love and pampering given to girls who could not otherwise afford a prom dress? Not only are they financially underprivileged, but some have been the victim of horrendous abuse, some have always been told they are ugly or fat. Some have become mothers; some have even committed crimes by the time they come to us.

The day starts with a plethora of volunteers, led by Amy Nance. Without Amy's love and leadership, the miracle would not occur. We are led in prayer by Dr. Phil. Smiling and organized greeters welcome the girls at the front door, where they are directed upstairs to the gym, which has been transformed into a magical fairy land.

Throughout the year, our church members shop for gently used formals. Some local stores donate new dresses. Even the men and boys have helped by setting up portable dressing rooms, and moving gowns to the shopping area.

A beautiful buffet has been set out for the Cinderellas and their families, who accompany them. There are busy alterations fairies, dress steamer fairies, and goodie bag fairies. I am selfish. I volunteer for the most fun job of all—fairy godmother. Fairy godmothers are the personal shoppers for the girls. We scour the racks of chiffon and satin until the girls find several dresses they like, then we accompany them to the dressing room to offer any assistance. Mostly, we love them and tell them they are beautiful and pray for (and with) them.

My first Cinderella last year was Sarah, a beautiful, delicate blonde with pale blue eyes and a cherub face. She picked three gowns. The first gown was a lavender princess ball gown with a diamond-studded floral top. She looked like an angel in it. When she stood in front of the mirror, she broke into a rapturous smile. Then, just as quickly, she burst into tears of joy. You see, it was her first prom dress, and at that moment she realized she was pretty. She knew she was loved. She knew she was worth the pampering.

More loving fairies were waiting in the shoe section, where we fitted Sarah for silver shoes, bending down to place them on her feet. Lastly, she chose a purse, necklace, earrings, bracelet and ring, all new and still in the boxes. When she left our loving care, she hugged me and thanked me. But her day was not over yet. Downstairs, her dress was steamed fresh, and she was given a bag of nail polish, makeup, and a framed Bible verse. I will not see Sarah again, but there will be other Cinderellas to love and lavish next year, and the next, and...

I Won Today

...We can rejoice, too, when we run into problems and trials, for we know that they help us develop endurance. And endurance develops strength of character, and character strengthens our confident hope of salvation. And this hope will not lead to disappointment. For we know how dearly God loves us, because he has given us the Holy Spirit to fill our hearts with his love.

Romans 5:3-5 NLT

He tried. Satan, that is. Yesterday, I worked at Twice Touched, a ministry for the needy. I hung donated clothes and unpacked and stocked food items.

Today, I paid. After a full day of activity, I require two days of rest, due to resulting fibromyalgia pain and fatigue. I was suffering extreme fatigue and pain this morning, but this was my day to be greeter. It was Sunday, St. Patrick's Day.

I had planned to go to church wearing my cheerful green dress, but it must have shrunk in the closet over the winter, because when I put it on, it zipped, but not if I wanted to breathe or sit down. And panti-hose. Every woman knows that panti-hose go on backwards at least 70 percent of the time. Then my slip strap broke, and I had to safety pin it. I found another bland outfit I could fit into, but then I had to change my shoes and jewelry.

The day was gray and the sky was dripping a drizzly rain. I felt like crawling back into my pajamas under the covers. But I don't like Satan. He did his best to foil me at every turn this morning, but I was stubborn. I persevered. I even made it to early Sunday School and enjoyed the sweet company of my sisters in Christ. Before that I was privileged to help a lady with walking difficulty to her class.

Soon, I was officially smiling at folks as they entered the sanctuary. Wearing that smile made me feel it in my heart. People are great. Satan is not. He lost today. I won. Praise God!

The Orchid

All men are like grass, and all their glory is like the flowers of the field. The grass withers and the flower fades, but the word of our God stands forever.

Isaiah 40:5-8 NLT

I bought the orchid in early April. It was on sale at Kroger. It was adorned with one perfectly unfurled purple blossom. Now, it was not fair to the beautiful plant that I should buy it, as I am a plant Kevorkian, but I was sure I could offer it a reasonably normal life. I googled "orchid care instructions." It said, "Cover the dirt with ice water once a week." For several weeks, I lovingly fed it ice water. The blossom fell off in season, but I was sure another would peep its purple head out next season.

It has been three years. The leaves still survive, but there have been no more blossoms. With the passing of time, my zeal diminished, so that for weeks I forgot to water it. From lack of care, one bright green leaf slowly yellowed, then fell off. I resumed watering, not as faithfully as I should, but enough to keep my orchid alive—barely alive.

And so it is with our zeal for our God. We start out on fire, a strong plant for God, then gradually we forget to feed with fervor, and we wilt. No more blooms. Still alive, but so needing the living water, that we cannot muster the energy to bloom. Our heart of worship becomes tepid or dries up altogether, so in neglect, we lose part of ourselves. Our soul dries and shrivels.

But we can bring ourselves back into glorious bloom. We can pick up the can and water our souls back to health with prayer, song, Scripture, and by reconnecting with friends who still thrive on God's word. With proper attention to our spiritual self, we can even blossom again, renewed, fragrant, and vivid in the eyes of God and those who need a little beauty.

Wild Animals *And* Angels

At once the Spirit sent him out into the desert, and he was in the desert forty days, being tempted by Satan. He was with the wild animals and angels attended Him.

Mark 1:12 NIV

Wild animals *and* angels, what a combination! Do you wonder what hardships Jesus endured during His 40 days wandering in the desert, as He prepared for His ministry? Could we have endured the cracked feet, breathed in the dry dust, remained lucid in the absence of sleep, squelched ravenous hunger, or survived the thirst with parched tongue, all in addition to the Satanic temptations He resisted? And wild beasts.

Read the last sentence of today's verse again. Pay careful attention to the word *"and"*. He was placed among wild beasts *and* angels. God did not cage the wild animals, which could have shredded Jesus's flesh and devoured Him, nor deliver Him from their presence. But He sent angels of protection, rendering the animals impotent in God's power. The beasts were visible and terrifying, the angels ministered, perhaps invisibly; both were real.

As we approach our 40 days of Lent with our self-imposed little deserts of deprivation, let us enter with humble hearts and happy faces, for the glory is soon to come. Thank God for the opportunity to sacrifice for Him *and* for the unseen angels attending us.

The Case Of The Climbing Clematis

If it is possible, as far as it depends on you, live at peace with everyone.

Romas 12:18 NIV

This is Holy Week, the saddest of days leading up to Christ's betrayal and crucifixion. Today I was accused by one of my country neighbors of stealing her purple climbing clematis. I was not even in the country on the day of the alleged theft. I bought my cabin for a peaceful retreat, somewhere to read my Bible, write devotionals, and pray.

Today my peace has been taken. I am upset; I am angry. I have been betrayed, slandered, and falsely accused. Wait! This week, more than 2,000 years ago, an innocent person far greater than any of us, was accused of far greater crimes by great masses of neighbors. Indeed, he endured the worst betrayal and suffered the most horrific punishment for those unfounded allegations—all for us. Was he angry? Perhaps. Was he sad? Deeply. But did he seek revenge or exoneration? No, he unquestioningly accepted his punishment, even offering forgiveness to his tormentors and to the very guilty, but remorseful, cross-mate hanging beside him, offering him a place in paradise.

Human betrayal is the hardest to bear, yet he bore it willingly. He did not protest; he did not proclaim his innocence. Mine is such a small betrayal. Jesus, help me bear it with dignity and grace, and to not seek quarrel or revenge, but peace with my neighbor as much as possible. Let me be more like Jesus. Maybe I'll even buy my neighbor a new climbing clematis, and take it to her as a peace offering.

Satan And The Red Shoes

Then he showed me Joshua the high priest, standing before the angel of the Lord, and Satan standing at the right side to accuse him. The Lord said to Satan, "The Lord rebuke you, Satan!"

ZECHARIAH 3:1-2 NIV

For weeks I had wanted the red flats I saw online, but I would not allow myself to buy them. Then came Lent. I gave up cookies and online shopping. By the end of the first week, I really wanted cookies.

Spring was coming, and I really wanted those red flats too. The past week I have endured a raging flare of fibromyalgia. I am improving, but still feel a little down. All the more reason to want cookies and red shoes.

Today, my friend sent me a devotional about the worst of all our enemies, Satan. It said Satan will hit you at your weakest, just like he tempted Jesus to make bread when He was famished after 40 days of fasting. It said to be watching for Satan to strike. Because he will.

As I was reading the devotional, those red shoes popped up in a colorful online ad. Because I was acutely aware of the kind of guy Satan is, I was able to click off the ad with little more than a glance shoe-ward. It was Lent, and I would not disappoint God. This day I chose the Lord when I was at my weakest. Today Satan did not fool me. I finished reading the devotional, and smiled. "Rebuke you, Satan!"

Peristeria Elata

After being baptized, Jesus came up immediately from the water, and behold, the heavens were opened, and he saw the Spirit of God descending as a dove and lighting on Him.

MATTHEW 3:16 NIV

It only blooms during Pentecost season, the Peristeria Elata, or Holy Spirit Flower. Some call it the White Dove Orchid. It is indigenous to Panama, which is why most of us have never seen a real one. I did watch a slow motion video of it bursting on the vine, transforming from ugly green balls into a cup of white petals, which then opened to reveal a long plume, which spread wide until its feathery wings opened to resemble a dove in flight.

How fitting, the beauty dormant until the resurrection and throughout the seven weeks, gradually emerging, until it bursts its wings into a glorious display of joy, like the first followers of Jesus felt as He was resurrected and poured His Holy Spirit upon them. The White Dove Orchid heralds the season with its white dove wings, as if ready to accompany our Savior up into heaven, year after year. So if you're ever in Panama, try to find one, and know that it was only God who could have created such a beautiful and timely symbol of resurrection and victory.

Like Mary On Friday

By Sara Garner

Standing near the cross were Jesus' mother, and his mother's sister, and Mary Magdalene. When Jesus saw His mother standing there beside the disciple He loved, He said to her, "Dear woman, here is your son." And He said to His disciple, "Here is your mother." And from then on this disciple took her into his own home.

JOHN 19: 26-27 NLT

It's funny how life changes your perspective. I've always loved Christmas much more than Easter. I've loved God for as long as I can remember—truly. I became a Christian and a Baptist at the same time, when I was 11 years old. I've never wrestled with the "why" of Christ's crucifixion. I have, however, been amazed that He would come to this earth at all.

During this season of Lent, my focus has been on Mary. As the mother of a precious eight-year-old boy myself, I see her sacrifice as so much more profound. I love this verse in Luke 2:19: "But Mary kept all these things and pondered them in her heart."

I wonder what this "day between" was like for her. The grief. The shock. The anger she felt toward Father God. The confusion. The anticipation: I love you people a lot, but I don't know that I would give up my freckle-faced tater for a single one of you.

As Pastor Bill Carter used to say on Good Friday, "But Sunday's coming!"

Nothing But A Cross

And anyone who does not take his cross and follow me is not worthy of me. Whoever finds his life will lose it, and whoever loses his life for my sake will find it

MATTHEW 10:38-39 NIV

There it stood upon a cold hill, one board down and one across, in the Alton Baptist Church parking lot on Easter morning. A little boy next to me asked his mother what it was. Absent-mindedly, she replied, "It's nothing but a cross."

"Nothing but a cross?!" I wanted to scream at that woman. "Blameless Jesus's hands and feet were cruelly nailed to such a cross for such a person as you. He was hoisted high to be mocked, taunted, and spat upon as He suffered in the scorching sun that awful Friday. How would you like that? How would you like a crown of thorns placed on your aching head, so that your blood dripped onto your tortured face? And how would you like to be parched and given vinegar, instead of quenching water? He endured all that for you and your little boy and me and every person in the world from then on. Would you do that for me, or even for your sweet little boy?"

Jesus hung high on that cross for the lowest of humanity. So next time you're grieving, tempted, or just weary, you have the comfort of that cross. You, yes you, can lean on nothing but the cross.

Romans 5:8

God demonstrates His own love for us in this: While we were sinners, Christ died for us.

Romans 5:8 NIV

We've all read it, memorized it, repeated it. Rote words. Today, I read it again in the *Upper Room.* Only this time it was all new. God showed me this message in a way I had never seen it before, emphasizing one word that literally seemed to stand out larger and bolder. DIED! I cried with the conviction of the sinner that I still am.

He DIED! My heart raced with both shame and gratitude. It was as if God was saying, "Do you hear Me? He DIED!" Not merely He passed, but the heartbreaking and miraculous truth that He suffered and DIED for us. For you. For me.

As I am writing, the church bells across the street are pealing "The Old Rugged Cross"—"For 'twas on that old cross, Jesus suffered and DIED, to pardon and sanctify me."

Say it now out loud: "Jesus DIED for me!"

Oh, Jesus, you have given us the highest love. You DIED so that we can live forever with You.

Hallelujah!!

Whispers

The voice of the Lord is powerful, the voice of the Lord is majestic.

PSALM 29:4 NIV

In an April Stephen Ministry meeting, Cleland read to us from a book by our own James Hale, titled *Quiet Spaces*. It spoke to me. It spoke of God's whispers. It reminded me that most of the time, God does not come to us in a tree of fire, a flash of thunder, or with a ton of bricks. God nudges us quietly through Scripture, Godly friends, devotionals, and the inner voices of our hearts. He speaks softly to us personally.

In the past, I have waited for the ton of bricks; they will come if we don't heed the whispers. What Cleland didn't know that day was that I was struggling with a moral dilemma. Yet for some reason, he handed me the book and told me to keep it. My messages were coming persistently, yet in a murmur. I had asked God for the right way, and He was answering—but I was not listening.

I was reminded of Dr. Phil's sermon about fake pearls. I knew I was settling for fake beauty, but it was from the one who wishes us despair. My God was gently offering me real joy and peace. I knew what my decision needed to be. It would be difficult, because it would mean the death of a lifelong dream.

When I opened the book, I discovered it was a 45-day listening-to-God devotional—just what I needed to get me through my difficult process. Then I knew that, not only would I make the right decision, but I would be swaddled in the love of God and my Christian friends.

I had crossed over in my walk with God. I was ready for real pearls. I was ready to listen. The next morning, my devotional reading was about, yes, God speaking in powerful whispers.

Washing Mother's Feet

Now that I, your Lord and Teacher, have washed your feet, you also should wash one another's feet.

John 13:14 NIV

My poor mother was a bitter, sharp-tongued woman. Life had not been good to her, but neither did she have the corner on adversity. We had a tumultuous relationship from my teen years until her death in 2005. She would spew venom at me, or berate my little sister, and I would storm out in anger and pain. I would stay gone for weeks until my heart softened, then I would go visit. She was always glad to see me, but she never apologized for her hurtful words.

Mother quit living when she was in her forties, but she didn't die until she was 81. In the spring of 2005, she was becoming more frail and forgetful. I felt an unexpected surge of pity for this unhappy person. One summer day, out of the blue, God told me to wash her feet. What a strange order! I didn't do it, and the promptings became stronger. How could I tell her I needed to wash her feet? Then, one evening she called me in a panic, which was not unusual, but this night I heard real fear in her shaky voice.

She had soiled herself, she said, and didn't have the strength to get her clothes off and clean herself. I went to her. She was indeed soaked down to her toes. I helped her out of her pajamas and cleaned her with a rag, dried her, and helped her on with some clean pajamas. Then I filled a pink plastic pail with warm water and soap. I dipped a clean cloth into the suds and gently washed her feet.

Clearly, God had dictated that I perform this act. I had ignored him, so he gave me this opportunity to fulfill his commandment. Mother died a few weeks later, and I will be forever grateful that I knelt humbly and washed her feet that night.

Memorial Day Red, White, And Blues

I will praise you, Lord, with all my heart; I will tell of all the marvelous things you have done. I will be filled with joy because of you. I will sing praises to your name, O Most High

Psalm 9:1-2 NLT

Here it was Memorial Day, and I had been cooped up in the house for two weeks with a bout of diverticulitis. I was in pain and tired. The air was stale. My cousins were having a picnic, and I couldn't muster the energy to go. I was starting to feel blue.

"I could at least get up and open the door," I thought. As soon as I did, my nostrils were greeted with the sweet smell of lilacs and the hickory smoke from a nearby barbeque. How delightful! I watched the vehicles come to a halt at the four-way stop sign outside my door.

As I watched, I decided to pray for each person that went by. A group of veterans on motorcycles sporting American flags, rumbled by. I thanked God for their bravery and our resulting freedom. Next, a white-haired couple in a gray Chrysler stopped a little too long before easing out into the intersection. I prayed that they had had a happy life together, and offered God my thanks for parents and grandparents. A young man wearing a bright orange t-shirt sped by in a jacked-up red truck with radio blasting. He didn't stop at all; in his youth, he was too much in a hurry. I prayed that he would have a fun day, and asked God to keep him safe.

I forgot about my pain for a while. My mood lifted. I realized I was breathing more peacefully. Maybe I couldn't go to the picnic this year, but I could see the blue sky laden with fluffy white clouds through the greening trees. I thanked God for His beautiful artwork. Then I hunkered down and drifted into a glorious Memorial Day nap.

H-O-P-E

And after you have suffered a little while, the God of all grace, who has called you to the eternal glory in Christ, will himself restore, confirm, strengthen, and establish you.

1 Peter 5:10 ESV

At the May 20, 2016 FUMC Prayer for General Conference, Elaine Stanovsky, spoke of hope leading to a more normal life, while we are in the midst of angst. A life without hope? Who could possibly want that—the defeat, the loss of faith, the emptiness, the depression?

Healing Of People Eternally—HOPE, she said. What if you lived your life without hope of eternal healing? Could you bear the earthly grief, physical pain, and misfortune all of us are bound to experience? What if it never gets better? That, my people, is a loss of hope.

But hope *is* our greatest hope. With it we can bear all things, we can stand strong in weakness, like Paul in 2 Corinthians 12:7-10. We can see beyond our suffering down the brick road to happiness and wholeness and laughter again. We will wake from our sorrows one beautiful morning and the sun will shine on our face. Even if our pain is never-ending on this small earth, our time here is only a blink. The life with hope *is* the normal life. And it is the gift that ultimately heals us all.

Healing Of People Eternally. Eternally, my friends, eternally.

The Garage Sale

The Lord detests lying lips, but He delights in men who are truthful.

PROVERBS 12:22 NIV

It was garage sale season. I lived on a street frequented by travelers coming off the interstate. About midday, a humongous RV trailer pulled up and stopped. Out scrambled two small children, followed by a middle-aged couple. They explained they were grandparents traveling from the children's home in North Carolina to the grandparent's home in Sedona, Arizona for two weeks.

The kids needed more entertainment than grandma and grandpa could provide. (This was before the days of cell phones and iPads.) They noticed a TV I had for sale for $25. They hauled it to the RV, then came back. They pulled from their wallet pictures of several more grandchildren, and engaged me in conversation about my town; I inquired about Sedona. We had a nice little chat. Then they said their good-byes and left. They had seemed nice enough, but they had failed to pay for the TV! Pretty slick, I thought, and chalked it up. On to the next customer.

Two weeks later, I was sitting on my front porch when the same RV pulled up and stopped again on their way back to North Carolina. The couple emerged with $25 in hand! With embarrassment, they told me how much they had enjoyed talking, and had only realized later that they had not paid me. This couple made a special trip off the highway to make good on their deal. As they drove off waving, I held on to that $25 and my faith in humanity.

The Ides Of June

I will give you a new heart and put a new spirit within you.

EZEKIEL 36:26 NIV

June had come in like the Ides of March—chilly, rainy, gloomy and blustery. Just when everyone had breathed an expectant sigh of relief that the brutal winter had passed, out came the sweaters and jackets they had so happily packed away the week before. People on the street once more scurried by, huddled in fleece, their faces glum.

Finally, the rain stopped, but the air was still uncomfortably cool. I sprinted across the street to put a letter in the mailbox, planning to retreat hastily back to the warmth of my home. Then I smelled it—the most wonderfully sweet fragrance! What could that be?

Looking around, I saw on the cold concrete, a large branch of a White Fringe tree, its leaves vast and verdant, its flowers white and fluffy. An ugly wind had snapped it from its limb and splintered its stem. I bent and picked it up. So soft to the touch, still alive, though tossed and broken. To me, it was beautiful.

I brought it home and placed it in my favorite tall etched vase. It perked up as if to say, "Thank you for rescuing me; thank you for noticing I was still of value." It rewarded me by filling my living room with the long-awaited sweet smell of summer.

And I wondered who was the luckier, the rescued or the rescuer? You know, it's like that with human souls, so hard to tell who is most blessed in the saving.

God And The Good Samaritans

But a Samaritan, as he traveled, came to where the man was; and when he saw him, he took pity on him. He went to him and bandaged his wounds, pouring on oil and wine. Then he put the man on his own donkey, took him to an inn, and took care of him.

Luke 10:33-34 NIV

Joanie, Cleland, and their 19 family members were so excited they could all get together to celebrate fun and love at Fripp Island in Beaufort, South Carolina this summer. We missed Joanie at church, though, and couldn't wait to see her when she returned. What we saw when she returned to us was horrifying. Her entire face was black with bruises, her lip was split, and she had a fractured right shoulder. She could barely walk. She told us the vacation had gone well until Thursday. While out for a stroll on the boardwalk, Joanie had tripped and suffered a nasty fall.

Immediately, a young couple in front of her raced to help her. An older couple behind them also ran to help. The young couple were both doctors, who rendered first aid. The older couple were their parents, who happened to have a wheelchair in their condo! They all helped Joan into the wheelchair and pushed her to the dock, where they waited with her until an ambulance arrived.

A bad fall happened at the right place that day. Surely, God had posted those good Samaritans near Joanie at the right time. In spite of the fall, God was in charge that Thursday on the sunny, sandy boardwalk.

What A Difference A Day Makes

The joy of the Lord filled the house.

Ezekiel 43:5 NLT

The weatherman had declared it meteorological fall a week ago. Still, stifling 90-degree temperatures lingered. Yesterday, Sunday, the 25th of September, was especially important to my church and the First Corinthian Church, because it was our annual joint picnic to be held in the local outdoor amphitheater. Our pastor debated whether to hold it inside, due to the "inclement" heat spell, but he was overruled. So his stubborn congregation sweltered and sweated into their potato salad as the thermometer reached a miserable 91 degrees.

Click! Switch to today—just one day later. As you went bounding out your doors this morning, you were greeted with, what? A chill! You were forced to scurry back inside to dig out your lightweight jackets and your socks. Maybe you even turned on the heat.

Being retired, I stayed home. I put away my summer shirts and traded them for a long-sleeved flannel favorite. Out came the hamburger, beans, garlic, tomatoes, spices and spaghetti, which would become my first batch of fall chili. I made peanut butter cookies, happily rolling the dough into balls, then dipping a fork in sugar and pressing criss-cross patterns into them.

The clouds came out, competing with the occasional burst of sunlight. Yes, it was unfortunate about yesterday, but today brings crisp air and cozy smells from the kitchen. My apple cinnamon candle is lit. There is glory in a quiet day. I am content and all is well with my soul. What a difference a day makes.

Crisp Green Apple

Grace and peace be multiplied to you, in the knowledge of God and of Jesus our Lord.

2 Peter 1:2 ESV

Have you ever bought one of those three-layered scented candles? Well, I did. Crisp green apple was on the top, next was salted caramel, and at the bottom was toasted hazelnut.

I lit that candle and soon an odiferous scent emanated. What had promised to be a delightful apple smell was instead a nasty rotten apple stench. When my kids walked in, even they asked, "What is that awful smell?"

I gave up on the candle and headed to the trash to toss it; but instead I grabbed a spoon and scooped out the melted green apple layer. To my surprise, the warm caramel wafted pleasantly into the air. What a cozy aroma! It made me feel like autumn and Thanksgiving.

I sit here in my living room now in the early October morning, enjoying the warm toasted hazelnut. And I wonder, do we ever treat new people like a green apple candle? The fellow on the corner might not smell so good, the new co-worker rubs us the wrong way. But what if?

What if we took the time and effort to peel back that first impression, instead of dismissing smelly apple people? What if, instead of tossing them aside, we offered them grace? We might find a warm, pleasant, loving person in the second layer of their being. And as we get to know them deeper, we just might uncover a delightful toasted hazelnut soul.

Veteran's Day, November 11, 2016

See what great love the Father has lavished on us, that we should be called children of God! And that is what we are!

1 John 3:1 NIV

Today is Veteran's Day. Some of us have been posting Facebook tributes and pictures of our fathers, only we still refer to them as "our daddies," even though we are grandparents ourselves. My daddy, Russell, would have been 100 years old this year. I couldn't bear to get his picture out today. My friend, Ellie, whose WWII daddy's name was Ralph, sent me the following e-mail today:

"I miss my Dad. Went to exercise class, and there was a little WWII vet there, wearing his military cap, like Daddy's, and I could not say anything to him. So he came over and sat on the exercise bike beside me, and we rode in silence to nowhere, tears streaming down my face, nose running. He finished, and I looked at him and managed a big smile. He did too. As he was leaving, the girl at the desk said, 'Bye, Ralph.' I think it was a God thing—a hug from my dad."

"I know it was, Ellie," I replied.

On Eating Tuna

Christians who are poor should be glad, for God has honored them.

James 1:9 NLT

We can be poor in spirit, poor in our grief, poor for being peacemakers. Even in our own poverty, we can give richly of our talents, gifts, time, hospitality, and encouragement. Perhaps some rich folks are more poverty-stricken in soul because they have chosen strife and love of things over a humble, grateful heart, like those who "drag us into court, blaspheming the fair name by which we've been called" (James 2:6-7). To these we can give our mercy.

This Thanksgiving after helping the needy, my own family, I have little left for my own cornucopia. So I ponder and smile at a poem by a kid named Jay Henze, who realized he was not as financially blessed as his more affluent friends:

> The rich eat ham,The poor eat tuna,Doesn't take as long to cook,So we eat soona'.

Jay was rich, because he possessed a spirit of thankfulness. I am rich today, because I have four cans of tuna and a thankful heart. Happy Thanksgiving!

The Thanksgiving Table

Give thanks to the Lord, for He is good.

1 Chronicles 16:34 NIV

The table was straight out of *Southern Living*, long shiny Mahogany. It was set with real gold-trimmed china and sparkling stemware. The dark green cloth placemats matched the napkins folded to stand up on the plates. The silverware was placed in proper order. The burgundy drapes hung luxuriously to the floor. The crystal chandelier shone elegantly over the table, casting a cozy, ambient glow.

That was someone else's table. Our Thanksgiving morning started with newspapers, bills, and medication bottles strewn all over the round oak kitchen table at Debbie's house. After coffee, the mess was scooped into a Vera Bradley bag and hidden in the bedroom. Real red and green Christmas dishes were placed around the table. Neatly folded green paper Dollar Tree napkins were put beside each plate. Then our silver-plated ware was set out backwards by me, the left-hander. Crystal? Hardly.

We were to entertain seven adults. Since we had only four matching glasses, we substituted two glasses with dog faces on them, and one with bold blue University of Kentucky insignia. Kayla's little wooden table was set with her special plate and a tiny ceramic turkey. The brown ceiling fan provided our lighting. Debbie and I started cooking the turkey breast, which refused to stand up in the pan, so we poked it in each side with forks for balance.

Next came—sweet potatoes. We forgot the sweet potatoes! Off to Kroger I ran without even brushing my hair. We finally managed mashed potatoes, green beans, Stauffer's macaroni, Stove Top stuffing, and, yes, sweet potatoes, all of which we served buffet-style straight from the cooking dishes. We did have homemade rolls. And a deli pumpkin pie with real whipped cream.

We took a picture of our "idyllic" Thanksgiving display and sent it to Jo, Dale, and Sophie, who could not be with us. Dinner was to be at one p.m. My crew—Chris, Chad, Jen, and little Kayla—arrived on time. Debbie's husband, Larry, and his mother, Naomi, who is 89 this year, were already there. Miraculously, there were no cooking disasters, and dinner was served by 1:15 p.m.

But first we stood in a circle, a circle of familiarity and love, holding hands, while Chris spoke the blessing. Then we grabbed our plates and dug into the buffet. The women did not wear pearls; we wore beads of sweat from happily cooking. We all wore jeans. But this was our version of Thanksgiving. This was our family gathered around, and this was our perfect Thanksgiving table.

Hydrangeas In The Snow

When the Lord saw her, His heart overflowed with compassion. "Don't Cry!" He said.

Luke 7:13 NLT

Every year we have a cousin's Christmas party. We eat, play silly games, then exchange cheap presents.

Teresa, Susie, Debbie, and I are the only cousins left. This would be an especially hard Christmas for Teresa, because her mother, Patty, had passed away during the year. Her absence at our party would be achingly felt this year.

We usually buy the same gift for each of our cousins. I was happy with the three large wooden Christmas bowls I had bought. This year, though, Debbie had shopped all year for just the right individual gifts. She was pleased with the English decorating book she had chosen for Susie, and the plush dancing red-nosed Rudolph she had picked for me. The gift she had bought for Teresa was a frosted glass candle holder in the shape of a branch with a cardinal perched on it. It really was the prettiest gift of all, but Debbie was not satisfied with it. It didn't "feel right."

Two hours before the party, she decided to go browse through a thrift shop. In the back, on the 75 percent off table, she found four ivory, gold-trimmed Lenox plates for 50 cents each! "Very nice," you might say, but these were special because in the center of each was a raised painted purple hydrangea! Again, you might ask, "So…?" *So,* Patty loved hydrangeas, and always had cut hydrangeas from her garden in the summer. Teresa missed that most of all about her mother. Debbie bought those four plates and hastily wrapped them. This time it felt right.

When Teresa opened them, she exclaimed, "Oh, these are mother's hydrangeas!" They made her cry bittersweet tears. What a miracle it was for a compassionate God to send Debbie to the thrift store that snowy afternoon for hydrangeas just hours before the Christmas party!

Christmas Eve Blessings

> *...The Lord's unfailing love surrounds the man who trusts in him. Rejoice in the Lord and be glad, you righteous; sing, all you who are upright in heart!*
>
> Psalm 32:10-11 NIV

Face book post by Doug Eades, 12/24/16

Thin mint cookies for Santa? Check.
Carrots for reindeer? Check.
Note telling Santa milk is in fridge? Check.
Prayers said before bed? Check.
Boys in bed? Check.

Lights low, surrounded by love and Christmas cheer. Now it's my time to prop my feet up, open a Blue Moon and listen to Lynard Skynard on the record player.

Blessed beyond measure, more than I could ever hope for. Grace overflowing, undeserved love, in sickness and in health, God provides for me.

The simple words, "Merry Christmas" don't do justice. They are so flippant, so misused, so commercialized.

My hope and prayer is that you—each one of you—will find joy. Break free of the stress. Let go of the shame. Turn the page on the pain.

You are loved and are worthy to be loved.

Peace to you, my friends.

Just The Thought

He who gives to the poor will lack nothing...

Proverbs 28:27 NIV

Kayla and I had done our Christmas shopping for her family at the Dollar Tree. She had chosen each gift herself—an odious pink candle for mommy, nuts for daddy, grandpa, and Uncle Chris, and a comb for Aunt Debbie. She had also helped me pick small gifts for the child I was sponsoring at church. This she especially enjoyed because the gifts were all items she liked—a ballerina skirt, a scepter and crown, a shiny candy-filled ornament, and purple gloves.

I explained to her that these were the only presents some little girls would get. She felt sad for the "little poor girls," but happy with her giving. She was learning the spirit of Christmas. When we got home, we removed each gift from the bag and were excited to think of how much each little girl would enjoy her gift. We wrapped (sort of) each gift and labeled it. Suddenly, Kayla announced she would feel bad if she didn't get any gifts for Christmas; then just as suddenly, her little face crumbled and she began to sob, huge tears flowing uncontrollably down her cheeks. Just the thought of finding no gifts at Christmas had broken her little heart.

It took several minutes of consoling to calm her. Then I began to cry. Every year I sponsor a child, but never have I really considered the true heartbreak of a child waking up to no gift at all on Christmas morning. The heart of my granddaughter had softened my own heart and opened my eyes to the harsh reality of Christmas without.

I don't have a lot, but I have enough. Next year I will do better. Next year I will sponsor more children. Next year I will really picture their little faces at Christmas, either crestfallen or joyous. If it is up to me, they will be joyous. Next year let's all do the same.

The Pitiful Tree

The city does not need the sun or moon to shine on it, for the glory of God gives it light, and the Lamb is its light.

Revelation 21:23 NIV

The little artificial Christmas tree was pitiful. Last year, it had sat regally on a table, but I had sold the table. This year, when I removed it from the box, it seemed to wither, especially when I sat it on the floor, all alone. Branches were huddled together. They seemed to protest when I pulled them apart.

Placing the tree on a chair gave it a modicum of dignity. Still, the white lights only sparsely covered it, leaving the rest to hide its nakedness. What could be done for my pitiful tree? Then I saw in *Good Housekeeping* a picture of a huge, tall tree, covered from head to toe in colorful lights. Lights—that's it! Off to the store I ran.

I bought 100 more lights, which I draped lovingly around my tree. That tree just, well, lit up! It seemed to stand taller and even looked fatter. The small ornaments twirled in the twinkling lights. I wrapped my maroon velvet tree scarf around the chair, giving my little tree a royal robe. Now it almost looked proud.

Next year, I might buy a pre-lit 7-foot-tall tree, but this year my little pitiful tree is not so pitiful after all. When I turn all the house lights off at night, my little tree stands tall and sparkles for me. If you are feeling withered and pitiful this season, cover yourself in the Light of the world. Then go out into the city and shine your light on someone else.

Behold...

By Debbie Smith

And lo, the angel of the Lord came upon them, and the glory of the Lord shone around about them, and they were sore afraid. And the angel said unto them, "Fear not, for, behold, I bring you tidings of great joy... For unto you is born this day in the city of David, a savior which is Christ, the Lord!"

Luke 2: 9-11 KJV

Night was lifting from above a magenta and midnight blue curtain as I drove through town on a cold, dark December morning. I was intent on delivering my toddler to day care and getting to work on time.

Suddenly, my breath caught in my throat and my heart started to pound! I couldn't believe my eyes, but there they were! ANGELS! I blinked. They were still there! What was...? The car quickly covered another hundred yards, and I then could see them clearly—larger-than-life wire angel figures entwined with tiny white lights. They weren't real! I breathed a sigh of relief, but also disappointment.

For an instant, I had shared the feelings of some cold, startled shepherds, centuries ago, when the Heavenly Host descended upon them, singing and sparkling in the black night: wondrous, illuminating, heart-stopping, breath-taking messengers of great news... but real!

Gold, Frankincense, And Myrrh; Cipro, Flagyl, And Penicillin

Their fruit will serve for food and their leaves for healing.

ECCLESIASTES 47:12 NIV

It's two days before Christmas. I have a UTI, and I just don't feel good. I am having trouble thinking of a miracle, when all I want to do is curl up on my heating pad. I can't get in to see the doctor until 2:30 p.m., so I will get a late start taking my antibiotics.

Antibiotics—that's it! That's my miracle! The three wise men brought baby Jesus the most precious gifts of gold, frankincense, and myrrh. The doctor will give to me an equally precious, even life-saving, gift this afternoon. One hundred years ago, before antibiotics, a simple UTI could have developed into a fatal illness. I take for granted that I will walk out of a very wise man's office with a little piece of paper, take it to another wise man, who will present me with bottles of little pills.

I will have no gold, no frankincense, or myrrh. (I'm not even sure what I would do with those offerings.) But I do know I will swallow my antibiotics with a big glass of water, and by tomorrow I will feel better. I will have the gift of health. What better gifts could God provide than Cipro, Flagyl, and Penicillin! Merry Christmas to all, and a Happy, Healthy New Year!

Midnight Miracle

Facebook post by Kari Williams, 12/24/16

And the peace of God, which transcends all understanding, will guard your hearts and your minds in Christ Jesus

PHILIPPIANS 4:7 NIV

While my theology is a bit eclectic, I am always awed and inspired by the peace I feel when I go to midnight church on Christmas Eve. I don't know that I necessarily buy into the whole story, but I know that I feel some connection to whatever Divine is out there. I don't know if it's the tradition, the family, connections with the past, the songs or the time of night, but I feel that, somehow, everything is okay. I feel peace and rest in ways that ordinarily escape me. I don't doubt that other people feel them in other religions. I don't doubt that their experience is any less important or legitimate than mine, but it's that, somehow, I find that peace that passes all understanding. For me, that's the miracle.

Midnight Magic

Janna Williams Smith, response to Kari's post, 12/24/16

For we were not making up clever stories when we told you about the powerful coming of our Lord Jesus Christ. We saw His majestic splendor with our own eyes when he received honor and glory from God the Father.

2 Peter 1:16-17 NLT

Kari, I always love going to the late service, too. Coming out after the service, everyone is so quiet! Sometimes you hear dogs barking, and I almost expect them to speak. It seems like anything can happen.

Anything can, Janna. Believe it.

For Unto You

After this his wife Elizabeth became pregnant... "The Lord has done this for me," she said. "In these days he has shown his favor and taken away my disgrace among the people."

LUKE 1:24-25 NIV

Zechariah and Elizabeth were old and without children. Then one day the angel Gabriel promised Zechariah that Elizabeth would bear him a son, who would be a joy and a delight. And soon John was born.

It all sounds so simple—one of the great miracles of life, the life-giving miracle itself. The angel's proclamation to Mary also described Jesus's birth as a joyful event. If you have ever given birth, or witnessed a birth, you have marveled that two people could create a tiny baby, fresh from the womb, who only a few hours ago you could not touch or see, but who now is waiting to be swaddled and laid in your arms.

This baby will not be perfect, like Jesus was. He will be full of snot and poop. He will spit up on you. He will make sure you have no sleep for at least six months. But the immediate, indescribable love you feel at his birth will only grow as he does. He will smile with joy as he recognizes your face, just as you smiled with joy when you first saw his face.

Soon he will drool and smile at the sound of your voice; you will swoon. Oh, like kittens, he will grow up, and there might be some tumultuous years, but this is your gift. God gave only you this particular little baby. Love him well, teach him right. If you are holding a new baby this Christmas, you are holding the most precious gift of all. God has looked on you with favor. God has told you there will be joy with this child born unto you. So rejoice! Joy to your world!

The Gift Of Words

Here is my advice: It would be good for you to finish what you started a year ago. Last year you were the first who wanted to give, and you were the first to begin doing it. Now you should finish what you started. Let the eagerness you showed in the beginning be matched now by your giving. Give in proportion to what you have.

2 Corinthians 8:10-11 NLT

Well, here it is January again. I started my blessing book in earnest a year ago. Each blessing story was to begin with a Bible verse. I intended to read my Bible, copy a daily verse, and write a story a day. How hard is that? But, today I reviewed my stories and realized I had written blessings for only 139 days! Where had the other 226 days gone? What was I doing that I was too busy to notice even one blessing a day, much less write it down?

Always the dreamer and procrastinator, I let time get away from me. Acknowledging my failing, I asked God to make me keenly aware of blessings around me, and give me the words and discipline to write them in a pleasing manner. Chris, my writer, has the gift, the words; but he also has the drive, and he writes prolifically. They say we should raise a child in the way he should go. That part is done. Now God has given me a lifetime full of blessings (sometimes in disguise) and the time to write.

So, I pledge today to turn the tables and be "like son, like mother," to take my inspiration from my child. God has blessed me with four new stories today, so today much is expected. Thank you for words, Father. May I gratefully give them back.

Kids

The Tomato

And hardworking farmers should be the first to enjoy the fruit of their labor.

2 TIMOTHY 2:6 NLT

I've never had much of a green thumb, but the second summer after Chad was born, I had dug a hole, carefully laid a scraggly tomato plant in it, and surrounded it with a cage. Then I tied it loosely and trained it up the wire. I watered it faithfully.

Soon, yellow flowers bloomed; like a miracle they turned into tiny firm, green balls. One in particular continued to grow larger, hanging heavily on the vine. I was proud! I anticipated the huge, red tomato it would become, and how I would pluck it, salt it and eat it raw, unashamedly letting the juices run down my chin—until the day Chad came to me, bearing a gift from his heart. With the unabashed pure love of a little boy, he handed me the unripened tomato, while proclaiming, "I pick it for you!"

Hiding my despair, I smiled, bent down and took it from his little hands. "Oh, thank you, Chad!" I mustered. His face beamed. He watched with delight as I sliced that tomato, then got the cornmeal and oil from the pantry. Soon it was sizzling in the iron skillet. When his daddy got home, I announced proudly how Chad had given us supper. We exchanged knowing smiles.

And that night, salted and peppered with love, we had the best fried, green tomato I've ever tasted.

Boy Healed

Then Jesus said to the man, "Bring your son here." As the boy came forward, the demon knocked him to the ground and threw him into a violent convulsion. But Jesus rebuked the evil spirit and healed the boy. Then He gave him back to his father. Awe gripped the people as they saw this majestic display of God's power.

LUKE 9:41-43 NLT

He was a tow-headed little boy, with huge brown eyes and ADHD. He struggled through school and with me, his divorced mother. By the age of 12, he hated me as much as I loved him. He was incorrigible and had begun having run-ins with the police.

Frightened, exhausted, and with a broken heart, I sent him to live with his father, a move I will regret forever. When he moved back with me, he was 15 and hated me more. He refused my hugs. Things got worse. He was violent. He had developed an alcohol habit and was suffering from depression. I feared that he would either kill himself or be killed in an altercation or an accident.

Counselor after counselor told us there was nowhere else for him to go, except to prison or the service. Praise God, he chose the service. He went away a bitter boy. I prayed and cried. I handed him over to God.

When he came back this time, he had changed into a fine man. He used his GI bill to put himself through college, then made a career out of the military, where he served in every conflict from Desert Storm to Afghanistan. He earned the Army Commendation medal.

He is now a loving son, husband, and the father of two beautiful daughters. He hugs me. Last week, he and Jen invited me to a movie. Last night, he asked me to fry pork chops, which I happily did. This morning, I received a text that simply said: "Meat loaf next time, best mom." I am still in awe and filled with joy that God gave me back my boy.

The Light On The Hill

Then Jesus spoke to them again, saying, "I am the light of the world. He who follows Me shall not walk in darkness, but have the light of life.

JOHN 8:12 NKJV

The situation had become hopeless. Seventeen-year-old Chad was slipping further into the deep pit of depression and rebellion. His anger was so great that he had physically assaulted me. Then he immediately sobbed, "I'm sorry! I'm not bad!" My endless love for him was mingled with a very real fear.

Police officers were at our home all too frequently. One night, an officer was afraid to leave me alone with my own son. The officer suggested I notify the military, where Chad was in the National Guard, and tell them of his aberrant behavior. In spite of the danger, I could not take from him his only hope, the possibility of a military salvation.

One night, Chad stood in our living room, his face filled with disdain, and asked me, "Why don't I just kill you?" I replied, "Why don't you? Then you can quit holding it over my head." Taken aback, he never threatened me again.

In fact, that moment was when the healing began. The only thing that calmed him was riding in the country. One Sunday, he agreed to ride with me to our farm. It was a quiet, tense ride; we had not much to say to each other. On the way to our farm, the Harvieland United Methodist Church sits on a hill—a tiny, non-descript, white wooden building, except for the stained glass windows. As we came over the hill, the setting sun lit up the tops of those stained glass windows, spreading shards of multi-colored splendor across an otherwise desolate day.

We both gasped at the beauty of the lights God had turned on just for us—at that precise moment, while we were alone together. We both felt the love of God and the depth of love we had for each other.

It is 30 years later. We still take rides in the country together, yet we have never seen the lights shine at that glorious angle again. We never mention the darkness that led us to the hill that day, but we always marvel at the light God shone on us.

In God's usual fashion, I opened my newspaper tonight and saw an ad for an event to be held at Harvieland Methodist Church. The ad referred to the church as "The Light On The Hill."

The Reprimand

You have charged us to keep your commandments carefully. Oh, that my actions would consistently reflect your decrees! Then I will not be ashamed when I compare my life with your commands. As I learn your righteous regulations, I will thank you by living as I should! I will obey your decrees.

Psalm 119:4-8 NLT

Chad has served in every military conflict from Somalia through Afghanistan. He has received several commendations, including those for his leadership abilities and marksmanship. He also received a reprimand.

In Kosovo, he carried his weapon in one hand and his Bible in the other. Chad spent his free time entertaining the children of Kosovo with volleyball games. He loved those unfortunate children. Every day, he took out his Bible and shared God's word and promises in simple stories with the children, who were otherwise without much hope.

A lone missionary in a secular military, he defied the orders not to share his Bible stories, and continued to offer comfort and knowledge of our God to those babies of a war-ravaged nation.

I thank God daily that he brought my son home safely after each conflict. I am proud of his sacrifice and accomplishments. I am proud of his compassion and his attempts to offer hope to the hopeless and knowledge to the unknowing. Most of all, I am proud of the reprimand.

The Blanket

Do not forget to entertain strangers, for by so doing some people have entertained angels without knowing it.

HEBREWS 13:2 NIV

I had seen the homeless man sitting in the wheelchair on the corner. I had passed him by on my way to work. I had said, "Good morning," but I couldn't bring myself to ask, "How are you?" I even doubted the wheelchair was necessary. Maybe it was a prop used to garner sympathy and perhaps a few dollars.

One cold, rainy night, Chad came in and asked me if I would make hot chocolate, which I often do for my children in the winter. He ordered it to go. He asked if I had an old blanket he could borrow. "Of course," I said. I would do anything for my children. He pulled the raggedy blanket from the closet shelf, picked up his hot chocolate, said, "Thanks, Mom," and left before I could hug him good-bye. Always in a hurry, that boy!

The next morning dawned, still wet and dreary. Complaining to myself about having to retrieve my umbrella, I trudged off down the street. On the corner, still sat the homeless man, only covering his lap was the blanket I had lent Chad. Over his whole body was a clear tarp that I recognized from Chad's truck. On the ground to his right, the empty hot chocolate mug rolled in the gravel with the wind.

My children. Those two words indicted my soul. I would do anything for my children. Yet this man was a child of God, and as such, a child of mine. I vowed to bring him lunch the next day, but when I got to the corner, it was empty. I had missed my chance to help a stranger. My child, however, had perhaps entertained an angel.

Go Woad, Get Whip Whip

For the moment all discipline seems painful rather than pleasant, but later it yields the peaceful fruit of righteousness to those who have been trained by it.

Hebrews 12:11 NIV

When was the last time you spanked a little butt? Or maybe you don't believe in spanking. How about the last "time out" you inflicted, not nearly as physical as a little swat, but excruciatingly painful in the mind of a busy preschooler.

Why did you punish your child? Was it out of anger? No, hopefully it was to teach your little one to avoid danger—a spoon in socket, falling through a glass door, falling off a ledge. These are all dire and immediate dangers we must save our babies from.

Young children learn by consequence. When Chris was two, he darted into the street. His daddy grabbed him just in time to prevent him from getting hit by an oncoming car, and delivered a hearty swat to his little Pampered behind. Chris was devastated. For a week, he went around our house, lamenting, "Go woad, get whip whip. Go woad, get whip whip." This was the only consequence he could understand. He had no awareness of the fatal consequences he could have suffered.

Speaking of suffering, his daddy suffered just as much every time he heard, "Go woad, get whip whip." He punished Chris out of love (and fear), but it hurt him to see his child in any kind of pain. And so it is with our heavenly father. He forgives, but He allows us to suffer the consequences of a foolish or sinful act, rather than leave us alone in our folly. Yet the earthly pain we feel when we have erred is nothing compared to the joy of entering the splendid gates of heaven for eternity.

Thank you, Father God, for forgiveness and consequences. Thank you for caring enough to grieve over your children, even as you correct us.

The Picnic Tree

Love and faithfulness meet together; righteousness and peace kiss each other. Faithfulness springs forth from the earth, and righteousness looks down from heaven. The Lord will indeed give what is good, and our land will yield its harvest.

Psalm 85:10-12 NIV

Behind our unassuming, white, shingle house stood an equally unassuming tree. Not a towering, majestic tree, but a tree just big enough to offer cooling shade to a mommy and her four-year-old boy. We dubbed it the picnic tree.

To qualify it as a picnic tree, we needed, well, a picnic, usually consisting of a soggy peanut butter sandwich, chips, and juice. Oh, and a blanket and a few books. On picnic tree days, I would pack our lunch, and we would climb over the rickety fence and traipse through the field behind our house until we came to our tree. Underneath, we spread our blanket and laid out our soggy lunch.

Sometimes we read Dr. Seuss; sometimes we lay back under the picnic tree and looked for shapes in the clouds. Some days we sang songs. Every day we went there, we laughed and cuddled. What a special tree!

Then came construction of a giant Kroger. We watched out the kitchen window as giant backhoes crumpled, then gobbled our picnic tree. Just like that, it was gone. Now the produce section stands where our tree stood.

I still remember that tree. We had taken a scraggly tree and made it something magnificent. We will never forget the tree, but we will forever have the love, laughter, and hugs we shared under our picnic tree. Nothing can take that from us, because, you see, love was what made our ordinary tree magical.

Wonder Woman And Me

Your beauty should not come from outward adornment, such as elaborate hairstyles and the wearing of fine jewelry or fine clothes. Rather, it should be that of your inner self, the unfading beauty of a gentle and quiet spirit, which is of great worth in God's sight.

1 Peter 3:3-4 NIV

When Chris was five, he was into *Star Wars* and action figures. With a shiny red curtain safety-pinned around his neck and Underoos over his pants, he staged fierce battles between Superman and Batman. But, alas, as it says in the Bible, man needs a woman. Thus, the addition of Wonder Woman. Posters of these heroes (and heroine) adorned his walls.

One day, as I was folding laundry, Chris came to me and earnestly asked, "Mommy, do you think you're prettier than Wonder Woman, or Wonder Woman is prettier than you?"

"Oh, I'm prettier than Wonder Woman," I replied. Being a five-year-old, he did not catch the nuance. He sighed and looked up at me with pity, as he left the room.

In a moment, he returned with his Wonder Woman poster. He had me stand in front of the full-length mirror as he unfurled the poster beside me. Breaking it gently, he said to me, "Now, look at Wonder Woman and look at you… Being pretty is fun, but being nice will get you toys."

Such sage advice from a little boy, such amusement for his mom. I'm sure being pretty is fun, and sometimes being nice will get you toys, but if not toys, then being nice will always get you blessings. Be nice.

Tennis Balls

For troubles surround me—too many to count!

Psalm 40:12 NLT

Chris was six and bad-luck prone. His brother routinely used him as an unwilling karate partner. He fell off the monkey bars and broke his arm. He stepped on a toy metal hoe, which flipped up and sliced his upper lip, requiring stitches. He slipped at the bowling alley and knocked out his left front tooth. He was plagued by wart-like skin eruptions, called mollusca contagiosa, which had to be burned off by his pediatrician. The acid marks looked like cigarette burns all over his little arms and legs. For a few weeks, I was hesitant to take him out in public for fear of being accused of child abuse.

Then he had a tonsillectomy, which didn't go well, resulting in a five-day hospital stay. In spite of it all, he never complained. Then one day, while playing in the back yard, he got hit in the head with a baseball. He came to me, holding his head, but still not crying.

"Next time I just want to get hit with a tennis ball," he lamented. The child didn't think to ask not to get hit at all, so accustomed was he to calamity.

Are you in a season of pain? Have you suffered a health scare, a financial setback, a life interruption, a failing relationship? These are all anxiety-provoking, but ask yourself, "Are my problems baseballs or tennis balls?"

Some truly are baseball severity; others are simply annoying or inconvenient. You, like Chris, are free to ask God to spare you. Sometimes He will; sometimes, for reasons only He knows, He won't. But try to put your problems in perspective. They might be just tennis balls, and you can be grateful for even that.

A Dark And Stormy Night

For we walk by faith, not by sight.

2 Corinthians 5:7 NKJV

Chris needed a ride to the airport 30 miles away; I was his ride. We left at 3:30 a.m. It was dark. It was cold. It was snowing heavily and horizontally. He drove to the airport. Then I was on my own.

Even in daylight, I am directionally-challenged. But in the dark, with the snow and the glare of other headlights, I became disoriented and took a wrong turn out of the airport. Off in the wrong direction I went. After gaining my bearings, at least I had the sense to know I was lost. I drove to the nearest McDonald's, turned around, and headed back home. Thank you, God!

Visibility was bad, and snow and slush left a dirty film over my windshield, reducing my vision even further. However, just in the line of vision I needed, there was a clear spot. Still, I white-knuckled it; still I was anxious. Then I cried, "God, please be my co-pilot. No! Please be my pilot." At that moment, my nerves calmed and my anxiety abated. I released my white-knuckle grip.

God drove me all the way home. Except for a premature turn into a mega-Kroger, we did just fine, God and I. All I had to do was ask, sit back, and relax in His care.

At The Intersection

Holy Father, protect them by the power of your name…

John 17:11 NIV

The first snow of the season came, looking as if God was sprinkling sparkly talcum powder over the land. The white was blindingly beautiful, but along with the white, came the black. What looked like shiny black onyx on the road was actually the malevolent and sometimes deadly black ice.

If you have ever spun out on black ice, you know the helpless feeling as you lose total control. My son was driving to work the morning of the first snow, past pristine silver horse farm fields. At an intersection, the light turned red. Chris applied his brakes, but his Honda went sliding right through. His heart pounding, he finally came to a stop and regained control of his vehicle.

The miracle was that all three other drivers at the intersection were aware enough to witness Chris' predicament. None of them took their right-of-way until they saw that my son was out of danger. Thank you, God, for undistracted, courteous drivers—and thank you for protecting my precious cargo.

Small Miracles

...for your Father knows exactly what you need even before you ask Him.

MATTHEW 6:8 NIV

Chris had been asked to give a national radio interview about his new book on Monday, 1/11/15 at 3:30 p.m., but had heard nothing further. When the day for the interview came, he was a bit disappointed. We watched a movie that was over at 3:25. When it ended, like every smartphone addict, he immediately checked his messages and found out he was indeed scheduled for the interview—in four minutes! If the movie had gone five minutes later, he would never have seen the message or answered it in time.

Usually, my rambunctious granddaughter would have been in my house at that time of day. On 1/11/15, however, the house was calm and quiet. Chris asked me what to say, as he had not had time to prepare. I advised, "Just answer the questions."

The phone rang and he began a flawless 20-minute interview. When he hung up, we both marveled at the events of that day. While we had sat unknowing, God had worked behind the scenes to make that interview happen, and we knew this sequence of small miracles was no coincidence.

A Stormy Day

When Jesus woke up, he rebuked the wind and said to the waves, "Silence! Be still!" Suddenly the wind stopped and there was a great calm.

Mark 4:39 NLT

It was a dark and stormy day. Oh, not outside. Outside it was actually a bizarrely sunny, windy 67-degree January day. But life that day was chaotic, and silent storms seemed to swirl in the warm air.

Chris was scheduled for hernia surgery early that morning. I had planned to bring him home and tend to him the rest of the day, but just as we were leaving recovery, Chad called. His ailing Dodge Ram truck had finally expired on a country road. He needed a ride home. Leaving Chris alone, I drove to pick Chad up. We made visits to various shady car dealers to try to find him a new (well, very used) vehicle. On one of our trips, I lost my phone. That entailed more running back and forth to places I might have left it, between trips to check on Chris. My mind was whirling with names and numbers of contacts I would have to reconstruct—if I ever got time to get to the phone store.

I sat down to catch my breath. There was an unfamiliar knock at the door. "What now?" I thought, as I wearily shuffled to the door. When I answered it, there stood my newspaper delivery lady—with my phone in her hand! While on her rounds, she had found it in the grass between the street and the sidewalk. I blessed her and offered to pay her. She refused.

It didn't occur to me until things had settled down that evening that, in the midst of my stormy day, a small miracle had occurred. I thanked God, placed my phone on the nightstand, and laid my head on my pillow, ready for a calmer day tomorrow.

Surrender To The Mystery

As thou knowest not what is the way of the spirit, nor how the bones do grow in the womb of her that is with child: even so thou knowest not the works of God who maketh all.

Ecclesiastes 11:5 KJV

The word mystery appears 22 times in the King James Version of the Bible. This tells us that God will not reveal our future like a cheap fortune-teller. He made us with inquiring, intelligent minds, but unknowing of His mysteries of life. And so we are left to wonder: Why do children die? Why is there physical pain? Why do tornadoes and floods destroy? Why is there evil?

How does God walk with each of us at the same time? How does the Spirit of God live in our souls? Why are we here? What happens when we die? How could God sacrifice his own son for us?

We will know only when we ascend to His holy mansion. Only then will we fully understand. Until then, as Chris put it, "Sit back and surrender to the mystery."

God is great!

Him

...And a little child shall lead them.

ISAIAH 11:6 ESV

(This was written by Chris in 2002. I copy this with some shame and a seared heart, as you will see toward the end.)

I first experienced a genuine body of Christians who love the Lord and seek to know Him and make Him known 10 years ago at a tiny Baptist church in the Kentucky hills. I had grown up going to church on Easter and Christmas, and had always assumed I was a Christian. But when I went to this church on the invitation of a friend, all my assumptions were shattered by a reality I never knew existed.

The preacher was passionate, people I had never seen hugged me and said they loved me, and I could tell they meant it. For the first time, vague, distant stories from the Bible became immediate, living Truth that shot through my soul. The Sunday school flannel-graph Jesus had suddenly become the Living Christ. I surrendered my life to Him there on a stormy Wednesday evening, and it has never been the same.

The first year and a half of this strange, precious new life was an experiment in letting go: alcohol, cigarettes, old friends. It was also a time of new discoveries: purpose, joy, wonder, and new friends in Christ who became closer to me than my own family. I decided to follow Jesus, and did not know that it would lead me from a youth group in Kentucky to a film studies program in Burbank to building houses in Juarez, Mexico. It's been a journey more heartbreaking and life-giving than I could have ever hoped for or imagined.

This journey has had its alternating rhythms of light and darkness, doubt and faith. In selfishness and distraction, I have taken my eyes off Jesus and suffered sin and disappointment. There have been moments when God was so close I trembled and others when I could barely scrape through a prayer. Times when I've doubted His presence and suspected His abandonment only to hear Him say, "Can a woman forget her nursing child and not have compassion on the son of her womb? Surely they may forget, yet I will not forget you. See I have inscribed you on the palms of my hands."

I believe that somehow, on a dark hill two thousand years ago, I was inscribed onto His hands and side and heart, and written into His eternal story. In recent years I have come more and more to appreciate this as an inexplicable mystery that words only attempt to describe. It is a message better lived out by a life of obedience and devotion to an unseen Master who is more real than the air we breathe. I daily try to read and meditate on the Bible, to seek God in prayer and to grow in the creative experience of living out His love and denying myself. I want to be faithful to Jesus. As part of this, I fellowship with other Christians and have opportunities to serve.

A few weeks ago, I was talking to my mom on the phone as she told me about her growing relationship with God. She told me, "Chris, I am saved by grace. I think I always was, but now I know it." This was the answer to a prayer I had started praying a decade ago when I was first saved by grace. And it was confirmation that the God who saved us both has never stopped listening to my prayers and working in my life, and that He never will.

Grand Kids

The Koi Pond

Have mercy on me, Lord, for I am in distress. Tears blur my eyes...

Psalm 31:9 NLT

When Sophie was two, her parents moved to a Texas border town. There was no green grass, just sharp brown stubble that pricked their bare feet. Dust and brambles blew around in the hot air. Their new neighborhood was lined with identical houses, made as if someone had taken one giant pastry bag, squirted them out in a nondescript row, then iced them in beige. The neighbors spoke only Spanish, which one could expect next to the border; still Chad spoke only English.

One day, Sophie slipped out the back door. In the few minutes it took for Chad to realize she was gone, she had disappeared. Frantic, he called for her, but she never came. He knew no neighbors to help him, and no way to tell which direction her little legs had taken her—to the front of the houses, possibly underneath jacked-up cars, or into the road; to the back, where many houses had unfenced swimming pools and unrestrained animals; left toward a power grid; or right toward a highway.

After running through several yards and yelling her name, he spotted her—standing at the edge of a slimy three-foot koi pond. She had removed her diaper and had her toes in the water, poised to jump in to a certain death. He walked as calmly as he could toward her, so as not to startle her. He scooped her up and held her tiny body tight, tears of fear and relief running down his face. "Thank you, God!" he cried. For he knew it was only God, who had led him, and just in time, straight to the koi pond.

Oh, Nothing

This is the day the Lord has made. We will rejoice and be glad in it.

Psalm 118:24 NLT

All moments are key moments, and life itself is grace. Frederick Buechner

"What did you do today, mamaw?" Sophie asked on the phone.

"Oh, nothing," I automatically answered. Then I began a litany of the mundane activities of the day. "You know mamaw has to vegetate and read her devotionals and drink her coffee first thing in the morning."

She laughed, all too knowingly. "Then I painted your bookshelf white. I did the laundry. After that, I took a big bottle of water from the freezer and took it with me on a drive to the farm to check on the new cabin. The drywall is up and now we can put the electricity in. It will be all ready when you come for your visit next week. I'm so excited to see you. I wrote a couple stories for my blessing book, then I watched an old Humphrey Bogart and Lauren Bacall movie."

"What is a Humphrey Bogart and a Lauren Bacall?" Sophie asked.

"Oh, never mind, funny girl," I laughed.

"What are you doing now, mamaw?"

"Just talking to you, Sophie."

Just talking to you? Did I really say that to my precious granddaughter?! Maybe this was an ordinary, nothing day, but talking to Sophie is more significant than anything I have done today. Ordinary days mount up to a life of grace. Thank you, God, for Sophie and our "nothing days."

Doug The Mug

But now, O Lord, thou art our father; we are the clay, and thou our potter; and we all are the work of your hand.

Isaiah 64:8 KJV

Sophie was visiting for the summer, so I enrolled us in a pottery class. We both spun, slopped, and slimed globs of wet clay into semi-recognizable forms—plates, vases and mugs. I must say hers were superior to my rudimentary results.

While she was making ring holders and Star Wars dishes for her parents, I decided to make a whimsical mug, with a face like those I had seen in those expensive pottery shops. The mug shaped fairly well. I rolled out two bulging round eyes and stuck them on the mug and painted them green. Next, I created a huge schnozzola and popped it smack in the middle of the face. I even poked tiny nostrils. Lastly, I rolled a thin strip of clay, fashioned it into a thin black mustache, and attached it directly below the giant nose.

Sophie and I waited breathlessly for two weeks for our masterpieces to be kilned and glazed. The finished pieces were not what I had imagined. I had grossly overestimated my talent. I really liked my mug, though—the not-so-gorgeous, yet likeable face staring back at me with a perpetually perplexed smile. I liked it so much, I named it—Doug. Doug the Mug. Not gorgeous George the Mug or monstrous Medusa the Mug, but just plain, good old average, unassuming Doug.

In a way, I was proud of Doug. I had made him with love, in my own image. But only God, with His unlimited skill, made you and me and everyone who has ever walked the earth. Some of us are physically beautiful;

some are average, but all of us are crafted by Him, who takes pride in everyone. I'm so proud of Doug that I poured sugar into his air head and sat him prominently on my coffee tray. How infinitely more proud God is of us, made in His image, displaying each of us as proudly as I display Doug.

Run To Mommy

The Lord says, "As a mother comforts her child, so I will comfort you."

ISAIAH 66:13 NLT

I babysat 18-month-old Makayla while her mommy and daddy went to the grocery. We had fun, cuddled, played peek-a-boo, and looked at books. She was happy enough. Yet when her parents came home, she burst into uncontainable joy at their return. She ran on tiptoes, shrieking with excitement, hands straight up in exultation. Jen bent down and scooped her lovingly into her arms. She rested her little head on mommy's shoulder, as if she was at last completely safe.

I could only wonder how marvelous it would be if we children of God could feel free to run without inhibition, with pure joy to Him. God never leaves us; we sometimes leave Him, but when we return, we should approach our Father with complete abandon. He will scoop us up every time, and we can rest our head on His shoulder, knowing we are loved in a way that no human, even a mother, ever can. He's waiting. Run. Rest your head now.

I Want You

You can go to bed without fear; you will lie down and sleep soundly.

Proverbs 3:24 NLT

Makayla is two. She has a nap-time falling-asleep ritual. Her left thumb goes in her mouth; she curls on her side. She pulls up the sleeve of the adult lying beside her and rests her feet on our plump bellies. Lastly, she simply says, "I want you." That's when she puts her hand up your stretched sleeve, and falls comfortably and calmly asleep. She feels utter safety in the presence of her adult.

Don't you sometimes wish you knew God so intimately? Don't you wish you could just pile up with Him and make your needs so plainly known. You can, you know. Three clear words, "I want you." That's all you have to say. Say them now. "I want you, Father." Now, close your eyes and fall asleep, safe in the sleeve of your Abba.

Harp Strings

Whenever the spirit from God came upon Saul, David would take his harp and play. Then relief would come to Saul; he would feel better and the evil spirit would leave him.

1 Samuel 16:23 NIV

My table harp used to be on the mantel. In my new place it sits on the floor, where the hands of a curious and musically-inclined 3 year old can reach it. And reach for it she did, but she missed, lost her balance, and fell on to it instead. Now some strings were broken; so was her little heart. She is a sensitive soul, and I could not bear to chastise her.

Gently, we lifted the harp upright, and I showed her how to strum the strings that were still intact. At the sound of her own music, her breath quieted and her tears dried, replaced by an ethereal smile. The beauty of a harp brings joy to the wedding, comfort to the dying, and peace to the mourning. That day, it touched a little girl's heart, making it a most magical instrument.

My harp sits back on the floor today, strings still broken, but tomorrow I will have them replaced. Then Kayla and I will play beautiful music, or at least make a joyful noise unto the Lord, not as beautiful as King David's but enough to soothe our spirits, and we'll both feel better.

God's Monkey Leash

Those who have never been told about Him will see and those who have never heard of Him will understand.

ROMANS 15:21 NLT

I live downtown, where Makayla could quickly dart into the street, so I decided to buy a leash, telling her it was a fun backpack. She picked out one with a pink monkey on it. The monkey on her back (pun intended) was there so she could enjoy her walks with mimi, and so mimi could relax during her walks with Kayla.

The leash part was because a three-year-old does not have the judgment or impulse control to safely walk the streets, and because a 65-year-old does not have the agility to chase after her.

The monkey leash was bought with love. God feels the same love for us. As new or even mature Christians, we sometimes make poor choices that can result in pain, if not outright disaster. We need a guiding leash of love. God wants us to enjoy the "monkey on our back," but He offers His gentle, non-intrusive guidance. He gives us the option of breaking out of our restraint, and He allows the consequences when we go astray. Yet when we are inclined to wander, God can tighten the reins if we seek His counsel.

When Kayla is older, she can graduate to holding my hand, then to walking alone. As we grow in our wish to live in God's will, we feel more desire to actually live within the bounds of God's grace, not needing the leash, knowing we are safe in God's plans for us. God, we thank you for your leash of love.

Ballet Shoes

Praise be to the God and Father of our Lord Jesus Christ, the Father of compassion and the God of all comfort, who comforts us in all our troubles...

2 CORINTHIANS 1:3 NLT

The week before her very first dance lesson, we took three-year-old Kayla to the studio to buy her leotard, tights, and tap and ballet shoes. She called her leotard her princess dress, and asked if she could wear it every day until dance time, but her teachers had told us not to let the children wear their leotards or shoes, except in dance class, so they would not be ruined.

The night of the lesson came. We helped her into her tights and princess dress. She put on her own ballet shoes. She danced around the living room, until she twirled herself into a potted tree. "I'm so excited!" she exclaimed.

Dance class was chaotic, but successful. Everyone was happy on the way home. Then came time to take off the ballet shoes. She became distraught; she was inconsolable. She took her shoes off and hid them behind her back. Who ever said taking candy (or shoes) from a baby was easy?

It took three adults to extract them from her little hands. Her tears were not of the tantrum variety, but heartbroken, snot-producing sobs. I was almost crying to see her so distressed. We were her tormenters. Still she ran to me, threw her arms and legs around me, and cried, "I love you!"

How could I hurt this child I love so deeply? Because I knew it was best for her in the future. When we are facing God's correction or living through a painful time, do we turn away from God, our Abba and protector? Or do we, in our brokenness, run to Him, even with sobs of the heart, pull close and cry, "I love you." If you are suffering now, why don't you run and jump into God's arms and rest? Tell God you love him.

But I Suck My Thumb

How kind the Lord is! How good He is! So merciful, this God of ours! The Lord protects those of childlike faith; I was facing death, and He saved me. Let my soul be at rest again, for the Lord has been good to me.

Psalm 116:5-7 NLT

Kayla is four. Her darkest secret is that she still sucks her thumb at night. Her secret is safe with me, her "mimi." Her sweet Aunt Debbie had invited her to spend the night, causing Kayla a dilemma. Her initial excitement was tempered with anxiety that her secret would be revealed. Tears welled in her eyes. Her first words on hearing she would stay with Aunt Debbie were, "But I suck my thumb."

"That's all right," I assured her. "Debbie is your family. She loves you no matter what. I think she knows already. She has penguin sheets ready for you on the bed, and she will sleep with you so you're not afraid."

Relief spread across Kayla's face like an open curtain. She began packing her pajamas and favorite toys for the fun trip to Debbie's. Her secret was out and we all still loved her.

Families are like that, you know. Families should love us no matter what. We can tell our families anything. God is our ultimate family. All our secrets and fears are safe with Him.

This morning, even mimi cried. I told God my biggest fear. He knew already. And He wraps my soul in penguin sheets, and he stays beside me. And it is okay if I cry. And it's okay if you do too. We're all God's children.

Hello, Kitty Thumb

The temptations in your life are no different from what others experience. And God is faithful. He will not allow the temptation to be more than you can stand. When you are tempted, he will show you a way out so that you can endure.

1 Corinthians 10:13 NLT

She's four. She knows better. I had told Kayla not to touch my razor. Yet here she came with a bleeding boo-boo on her thumb. When I asked how it happened, she evaded my question.

Into the bathroom we went to retrieve the Hello, Kitty band-aids from the medicine cabinet. She whimpered a little when I placed it over her thumbnail. Worse for her, though, was that the injury was to her right thumb—the thumb she sucks. Nap time came. Without thinking, she stuck the Hello, Kitty thumb into her mouth. She took it out and tried again, but she just couldn't suck a band-aided thumb. It was quite the inconvenience for a little girl, the result of a poor choice.

How many times has God warned us in love to stay away from a situation, and how many times have we ignored Him, and barged right in? And how many times have we suffered the consequences? Yet, whether a result of correction or natural consequences, we suffer, or worse, we cause someone else to suffer. Maybe the punishment is just a minor inconvenience. Yet in our disobedience, we can ruin marriages, jobs, finances, or health. So stay away from life's razor blades. Heed God's loving admonitions. It'll save you lots of boo-boos.

There's Daddy!

And by him we cry, "Abba, Father."

Romas 8:15 NIV

Yesterday was Kayla's first trip to our farm. Mommy was working, so Daddy and I drove her out to my place in Bald Knob, Kentucky. She complained of a tummy ache as he drove the 12 mile curvy road, not sure she wanted to go, not really sure she knew what a farm was. She's a city girl.

When we rounded the last curve and pulled into the gravel driveway beside the long flat green pasture, she was still confused because, at that time, there was no house. She stood in awe at the edge of the field, but did not move. We explained that this was her farm and that she could run, run, run as far as she wanted in the soft grass.

So she did. Dark hair blowing in the wind, she took off with abandon. She twirled until she fell into a heap, then did it again. She somersaulted. She teasingly ran from her daddy, until he caught her and swept her up in his safe arms, both laughing, falling to the ground, and rolling in the weeds.

So caught up was she in her freedom, that she forgot her daddy was with us. She hadn't noticed as he walked down the field, surveying the tree line. Stopping in mid-twirl, she noticed him. "There's Daddy!" she cried happily, as if seeing him for the first time.

Sometimes in our joy or sorrow, or just busyness, we forget our Heavenly Father is with us. He is never out of our sight, but it is we who cease to see His presence. Yet, like an innocent child, we can feel the joy again the instant we look up, and cry, "There's Daddy!"

The Gift Of Quietness

When He giveth quietness, who then can make trouble?

Job 34:29 KJV

Yesterday He did not giveth quietness. Oh, how I longed for it! Entertaining a four-year-old does not involve quietness.

It began at 5:45 a.m., when I heard a little voice whisper into my ear, "Mimi, can I get up now?" I = We. I deposited her on the couch with a pillow, a warm blanket, and Cartoon Network. I stumbled to the kitchen, switched on the coffee, fumbled with the Swiss Miss package, and fixed her a bowl of Froot Loops. Back to the living room I trudged.

What a fool I was to think that child would still be lying quietly on the couch! Papers and crayons were already scattered. "I want apple juice," she announced. No time for a sip of coffee, so back to the kitchen, with little feet pattering behind me. "Can we paint now?"

A red and white plastic table cloth adorns my new dining room table, ready for such art projects. I retrieved 12 colors of paint, brushes, and water. Miraculously, only the purple bottle spilled all over the floor.

Ten minutes later: "I want to make my jewelry now." Out came the jewelry set with string and 10,000 beads, 8,000 of which landed on the floor. Mercifully, that lasted 15 minutes—long enough for me to down a few gulps of caffeine.

Surely it must be noon, I thought. I glanced at the clock: 6:30 a.m. And so the day went, until her daddy picked her up at 5:45 p.m. Twelve hours, non-stop.

After I kissed her good-bye, I crumbled into a pile on the couch, too tired to do anything but stare at the carnage of toys she had left behind.

Today God has *given* me quietness. The word *given* stands out. A *gift*, a respite from the loving ravages of a 4-year-old. A chance to spend time with Him, a time to read or write. Yes, a blessed *gift*. I savor it, breathe it in, and take a slow sip of coffee. Ah, the *gift* of quietness.

Six-Eyed Santa

There is one God, the Father, by whom all things were created, and for whom we live.

1 Corinthians 8:6 NLT

It was to be a simple art project. Take one unused paint brush. Paint it red on the handle, white on the bristles to start a Santa Claus face. Kayla accomplished this part with no disasters. Lastly, place two plastic eyes from the craft store to complete Santa's face. She chose two eyes from the bag, and placed one directly in the middle. Then, one by one, she glued five more eyes straight up the handle. Debbie and I watched in bemused horror, as that jolly Santa was transformed into a six-eyed Cyclops.

We at first gently attempted to persuade her to place just two eyes, side by side, but her creativity had run amok. Admitting defeat, we both managed a "Good job, Kayla!" She was proud. She happily showed that six-eyed Santa to her mommy and daddy, who looked at us with a twinkle in their eyes and uttered their own enthusiastic "Good job!" We all knew it did not matter that Santa had six eyes; it mattered that a four-year-old had fun with her family and felt pride.

Maybe next year we will try for a two-eyed Santa, but this year, happily displayed on the wall is a strange Picasso-esque creation, only slightly resembling Santa. Our project did not turn out as planned, but plans often don't. If things are going a little awry for you, just imagine a six-eyed Santa, smile, and wait a while.

The Chaos Of Love

Father to the fatherless, Defender of widows—this is God, whose dwelling is holy. God places the lonely in families...

Psalm 68: 5-6 NLT

The grandkids and their parents descended upon my peaceful dwelling and swooped it into a chaotic frenzy. They stayed three days, enough time to completely annihilate my clean house. Toys were strewn, orange juice spilled, crayons lost. Play Doh and brownies were smashed into the carpet. Shoulders banged into shoulders, as we made our way through my shotgun house. I was ready for quiet and a tidy home.

Today, they all left. I have my quiet—and here I sit. It really didn't take as long as I thought it would to clean all the messes. The floor is swept and Swiffered; the carpet gunk is removed. Everything is neatly back in place. Today, I have what I longed for yesterday—peace and calm. And I am a bit lonesome, even though I know they will fly back to my nest soon enough.

Today, I ponder those sitting alone in nursing homes or lying alone on their death bed. Through my momentary solitude, God is increasing my calling to go sit and chat with the nursing home grandma, and to hold the hand of the dying man.

How fortunate we are to have family to love and disrupt our calm. How incumbent it is on us to spend time with those who don't. Ooh, I just stepped on a melted glob of candy, and for that I am grateful. Father of us all, Leader of the family, I am grateful.

With Love Comes the Mourning

With Love Comes The Mourning

And now the three remain: faith, hope and love. But the greatest of these is love.

1 CORINTHIANS 13:13 NIV

This morning, I was reviewing the Rainbow Study Bible Color Code Guide, which gives key subjects in the Bible and where to find them. I came to the green block titled LOVE. Love was described as joy, kindness, mercy, comfort, compassion, peace, sympathy, humility and charity. Love was also described as mourning and lament. Love involves all those happy, peaceful traits. Yet true love involves the risk of loss through illness, death, or betrayal. It involves our own pain and suffering, but worse, watching our children or loved one's suffering.

Tears and broken hearts are part of loving. True, but to avoid the mourning, we must also forego the love. To go through life with a dead heart is a far greater tragedy than to mourn. What a loss that would be!

The happy descriptions of love far outweigh the sad words. If we open ourselves to love, we must also be willing to accept the wrenching sorrow that might come with it. But, oh, the joy, when the season of mourning is over! To experience love in all its wonder and awfulness is to be alive.

December 18, 1998

I am the light of the world. If you follow me, you won't have to walk in darkness, because you will have the light of life.

John 8:12 NLT

December 18, 1998 was a dreadfully dreary Friday. "How can you recall that?" you might ask. Because it was the day we found out.

My office on Broadway was in the front of my home. I was taking a break in the back kitchen, chatting with my secretary, when Tom walked in, which was odd, because he was a lawyer over on Main Street and should be in his office.

He asked my secretary to leave. Then he sat down with me at the table. He had been to the doctor that morning, he began, and had been told he had lung cancer, Stage IV, with metastasis to the adrenal gland. Calmly, almost detached, he relayed that devastating news.

Because of his calmness, it took a moment for the reality to set in. The doctor had recommended no treatment, and had gently told him to go live out the estimated eight months he had left.

I felt like someone had hit me in the chest and knocked my breath out. I did not cry; I could not cry. He wanted first to visit his dad, who was buried on a cold hill in the Lebanon Cemetery. We drove there and stood with a freezing wind attacking us, as he "talked" to his father.

Next, we went to his mother's house, where he began by saying he had some bad news. "Oh, I hope it ain't cancer!" she seemed to beg. It was cancer. She cried; I still did not.

I don't remember much about the rest of that day, except that we decided to move our planned January 1999 wedding to December 20, 1998, only two days away. He first offered me an out. I told him if I were going to promise "to love him in sickness and in health, till death did us part" two weeks from now, I would do it two days from now. I meant it all the more urgently now. And so began our journey into sickness, but we had each other and God would see us through.

The Wedding

You thrill me, Lord, with all you have done for me! I sing for joy because of what you have done.

Psalm 92:4 NLT

Tom and I had been together for five years and had recently decided to get married. It was a happy time. He had given me an antique diamond ring. I had bought a long, classy, ivory skirt with matching beaded top. My sister had purchased her teal maid of honor dress and my nieces their purple one-strap bridesmaid's gowns.

The wedding was set for January, 1999. On Friday, December 18, we were told Tom had inoperable cancer, and that his life expectancy was eight months. He offered me an out. I refused it. And so we got married in the Crestwood Baptist Church at two o'clock in the afternoon on Sunday, December 20, 1998.

Because Tom was an attorney, we were able to get into the courthouse on Saturday and obtain our marriage license. All day Saturday, we phoned friends and invited them to our "shotgun wedding." Folks came with tears and heavy hearts, but Tom would have none of that, he told them. "Today is to be a happy day, a happy day for Vicki," he admonished.

We had had no time to decorate, but the church had been decorated with a large mural of Bethlehem and a brilliant display of red poinsettias with ivory velvet ribbons. Since there was no time for a cake, Chad and Jen offered the topper from their wedding cake the year before, with the frozen-in-time plastic bride and groom decoration still standing. It was too late for a florist, so my sweet sister drove to our farm and picked me the most precious winter bouquet of greenery and dark red berries. She also beautifully sang a song I had written for the wedding. My white satin shoes were not yet dyed to match my outfit, so I wore them slightly "off color."

A venue for our reception was totally out of the question—until Tom's friend and his wife, who lived in a mansion in horse country, gave us a reception as a wedding gift. They both stayed up all Saturday night decorating and preparing a feast for us. A glittering tall tree and shining silver greeted us when we walked in the door. Someone (I still don't know who) had ordered a limousine to take us there.

We celebrated our union into the night with our dearest friends and family. This was our day, bittersweet, but more blessed and beautiful in its circumstance—one of the most special days of my life. Oh, and we had another two and a half years until death did us part.

Cardinals And Other Angels

I will never forget this awful time, as I grieve over my loss. Yet I still dare to hope when I remember this: The faithful love of the Lord never ends! His mercies never cease. Great is His faithfulness; his mercies begin afresh each morning.

LAMENTATIONS 3:20-23 NLT

When Tom was dying of cancer, a picture of a cardinal on our mantel became our symbol of comfort. He died 7/2/01. Shortly after his death, cardinals began to appear in the strangest of places, always in my direct line of vision, hovering as if to say, "Do you see me? I am fine. I am here for you!" Then they would flit away.

During a trip to visit my son in California in 8/01, I looked out the stone motel window, and there sat a crimson cardinal on the windowsill, in the middle of the concrete jungle that is Los Angeles, where there are no nesting trees. Even now, if I am struggling with a hard decision or just feeling blue, a cardinal will appear. Last night a cardinal darted from a bush and flew across my windshield, as I was driving down a country road, pondering a large purchase.

Tonight, I was reading stories of mourners seeing cardinals after the death of a loved one— awe-inspiring and mysterious sightings. Two separate people said they lived in California, and would love to experience the sight of a cardinal, but there are no cardinals in California. Oh, but there was! At least one on that high cinderblock sill. Now I am even more convinced that God sends these cardinal angels to soothe our souls. Call me crazy, but call me comforted.

May you come to find comfort in and remember
Cardinals appear when angels are near.
So go now, sit outside, and drink your tea.
Keep a look out for the little Red Bird.
It's there your loved one will be.
Author unknown

But Then, The Vulture

Do good to those who hate you, bless those who curse you, pray for those who mistreat you.

LUKE 6:28 NIV

If cardinals are sent by God for peace and solace, doesn't it make sense that He could send warnings of evil? As Tom approached death, his family refused to accept that he was dying, so they blamed me. They turned on me with a vengeance. I was totally blindsided and unable to believe their abuse was intentional. However, when I was physically attacked by Tom's mentally ill daughter, and his mother grabbed my cell phone, so I could not call for help, I had to accept the intentionality of their behavior. (I have since learned from Hospice that this behavior occurs in families. They need someone to blame for their grief, so they will pick a "whipping boy." I was that "whipping boy.")

Hardest to take was the betrayal of Tom's brother, Don, who had accepted the wishes of Tom and me, until he fell under the spell of his domineering mother. When Tom's best friend and power of attorney, passed away suddenly two weeks before Tom, Don put a pen in Tom's hand even though Tom was in a coma, and forged his signature, making himself the power of attorney. "Tom _______," it said. Tom always signed his name, "Carl T. _______."

When Tom died at 11:18 a.m. on 7/2/01, I was the only person with him, except for the Hospice nurse. No other family members kept vigil. The day Tom died was the last day I lived in the house. When I returned later to retrieve my clothes, Don had put them all in garbage bags and thrown them on the floor.

Don inherited Tom's farm. He was later arrested for growing marijuana on this beautiful piece of land. His farm is on the way to my farm. My farm soothes my soul. As I passed his farm a few days after Tom's death, a vulture carrying a dangling dead snake flew so close to my windshield that I was terrified the snake would fall directly in front of my face. I felt true revulsion and dark evil. I have never before or since experienced such a vile sight. Evil does exist. Be aware that God warns us, and heed the warnings, but know that God's love abounds. Good will prevail. Choose good.

The Paradise Of God

Where, O death, is your victory? Where, O death, is your sting?

1 Corinthians 15:55 NIV

Shortly after Tom's death, following his long battle with cancer, my dear friend, Barbara, piled me into her dark green convertible and took me on a trip to the Outer Banks. We decided to make it a "God trip", intentionally noticing the beauty of God's creations around us. We travelled the back roads, visited Mayberry, ate Vienna sausages and crackers in front of a white clapboard church. We found a charming motel that led straight out onto a secluded beach. We climbed seven lighthouses and stood even with the tops of the pines.

One sunny day, we visited an empty amphitheater, and being local actresses back home, we performed an improv routine on the stage. We met a man named Peter on a boat. A woman with terminal cancer and a great spirit welcomed us to her church in Ocracoke. We ate lobster in an enchanting outdoor restaurant overlooking the bay. The water was serene, cerulean blue, dotted with diamonds of sunlight. Fishing boats and canoes in primary colors punctuated the landscape. Above, the sun smiled happily at us, covering us with a golden warmth.

For a moment, I felt sadness that Tom could not see this splendor. Then I realized Barbara and I were seeing only an infinitesimal glimpse of the paradise of God. Tom had overcome. The beauty he was seeing was spectacular in ways I could not imagine. He was eating from the tree of life, at the right hand of God.

I ordered a big piece of (almost) heavenly key lime pie and smiled upward.

The Signs

Rescue me, O Lord, from evil men; protect me from men of violence.

Psalm 140:1 NIV

(This story is an embarrassing one, but I share it in the hopes that it can save even one woman who is experiencing The Signs.)

Four years after Tom's death, I met a man. Only too late did I discover the signs. I had heard about such men in textbooks, sociology class, and the news. So I should have known. He came into my office collecting for a charity. Good guy points. He was charming and witty, besides he was a beloved sports figure.

Sign 1: He came on strong.

Sign 2: He drank a little too much. With an uneasy feeling in my gut, I married him after a short, pressured courtship. Day one of marriage: no red flags. Day two: We travelled to NY to attend my son's wedding.

Sign 3: He disappeared after dinner. The kids found him passed out behind a dumpster. When he returned to the motel room, it started in earnest, the screaming, the wild accusations. I realized that he was straight out of the textbook on domestic abusers, but I had made my vows.

Sign 4: When we got home, it escalated. He would spend hours in his "workroom," where I later found the stash of vodka and marijuana.

Sign 5: Valentine's Day. I prepared a roast, carrots, and potatoes, and put a rose by his plate. As usual, he was late coming upstairs. When he did come up, he was on a rant. There was no provocation; he just chose to rant.

Sign 6: Before the night was over, I found myself humiliatingly blocked in the closet by his massive form until I would say his name.

Sign 7. Then he stole my car keys, so I couldn't escape, and he went and sat in a darkened room, brooding.

Sign 8: When I called the police, he told them I had been drinking. I do not drink. After determining my sobriety, the police rescued me from that house of horrors.

Sign 9: It was not over. The stalking, legal wrangling, break-ins, threats, and hands around my neck began. Still, I would (and did) risk dying to escape such evil. If not for the love and physical help of my friends and family, I could not have escaped. That is the miracle for me.

It can happen to anyone, at any socioeconomic level, at any age. The rescue and its aftermath will be frightening. Get out anyway. I tell you this as a cautionary tale. Maybe my story is the miracle for you. Maybe it will save you. Heed the Signs! Run!

Planting For The Lord

Whatever you do, work at it with all your heart, as working for the Lord, not for human masters, since you know that you will receive an inheritance from the Lord as a reward. It is the Lord Christ you are serving.

Colossians 3:23-24 NIV

So, as is the case with an abuser, the torment continued after I left—the stalking, the breaking into my home and standing over me with his big hand around my neck, threatening "I can crush your neck in 3 seconds," the prolonged legal maneuvering that ate up a small sum I had inherited from my mother.

He and I still owned a house (not a home) together, which we had for sale. Perhaps the cruelest trick of all was that he convinced the court to order me to plant flowers in the yard of that house of horrors to increase the curb appeal. If I refused, he would think of other diabolical wounds to inflict.

So one Saturday, I went back to that place, got down on my knees, and began to plant geraniums while I cried. I looked up and there he was parked in the cul-de-sac, sneering. I could not let him know I was crying, so I pretended my tears were sweat. It was the ultimate degradation.

At Sunday school the next day, I told the story of the flowers. My sweet teacher, Martha, suggested I plant the flowers, not for my tormentor, but for my savior God. Then they prayed for me. The next day, as I planted, my heart was lighter. It was so much easier to plant for the Lord. Experiencing God was taking place—the book, the friends, the prayers, the church, the word, and the circumstances. I was the one down on my knees, but God was holding me up. My eternal inheritance will come.

Every Thorn Has A Rose

And after you have suffered a little while, the God of all grace, who has called you to His eternal glory in Christ, will Himself, confirm, strengthen, and establish you.

1 Peter 5:10 ESV

I was strolling down the country road, lost in thought. The air was sweet with honeysuckle and lavender. I breathed it all the way in. The marshmallow clouds moved swiftly across the teal sky, beckoning me to come along.

In my mind, I was choosing the cloud I would lie on and drift up to the heavens. That's when I felt it—a sharp pain that pierced my right forearm. The thorn. When I tried to pull away, it dug deeper into my flesh. I knew it would hurt most when I pulled it out, but pull it out I must. I stopped in the road as it dragged me back. I reached down to extract it. Only then did I notice the delicate coral wild rose on the bush. Its beauty made me forget its prickly thorn.

One painful pull and I was released from the stinging grip and free to revel in the loveliness of the petals. Knowing now to avoid the thorns, I reached down and carefully picked the fragrant rose. Back home, I put it in a tiny, clear glass bottle and sat it in my kitchen window. Three days later it still kindles happy thoughts. The thorn was only a small price to pay for the lingering joy of the coral rose.

Everyday Miracle People

Baby Taken

Written May 30, 1967

The Lord is close to the brokenhearted and saves those who are crushed in spirit.

Psalm 34:18 NIV

I never knew him, but they tell me he was a sweet little angel,
As he is now.

A round cherub mouth, a dimple poked into his chin,
And crimson ringlets haloing his precious face.

What a fighter those fiery curls would have made him!
Yet he had no chance to fight.
He entered and left
And never knew.

What would he be today? Almost a man,
Yet still a child.
Leaving frogs behind for girls,
Playing football and racing engines.

No. He was denied a little boy's impish grin,
An adolescent rebellion,
And the stature of a man.

He was only one second in an eternity,
Yet no minute could be complete without him.

I like to think that God's eyes
Deemed him too precious
To live outside of Heaven,
And so gave him back the life
We wait for now.

God's special son
And my only brother.

The Day After

And now, dear brothers and sisters, we want you to know what will happen to the believers who have died so you will not grieve like people who have no hope.

1 Thessalonians 4:13 NLT

The sun is shining, but a sad, gray pall covers the grass and flowers. The day lilies are still orange, but not vibrant. The hydrangeas are a faded lavender. Hippies stroll by, happily unaware, carrying their eco-friendly bags, filled with God's provisions from the Farmer's Market— plump tomatoes, fresh corn, pungent onions. Yet today they would be tasteless and bland in our mouths.

Last night, after a five-year intermittent illness, Ashley McClure left this world. Come to think of it, maybe that's why only the sky is a vivid blue this morning, no clouds, just happy heaven. Why she suffered so long, only God knows. Why her parents and sister had to endure the horror of watching their beloved Ashley wither in body is too heartbreaking for us down here to fathom.

A few years ago, Ashley promised that even if she could do nothing else, she would still pray for others. She kept that promise. Only a few weeks ago, she posted that she was home from three weeks in the hospital, and enjoying lounging by the pool. Hardly a mention of her pain, but thankful for her one day in the sun. Then another setback.

Then last night. So, we go about our day today with broken hearts, but heaven is singing. Maybe Ashley was too good for this world, so God came to get her and softly lifted her away in her sleep—to love and wholeness and beauty only heaven can manifest.

Ashley McClure, precious child of earth for a few, short years. Ashley McClure, precious angel of God for eternity. Our incomprehensible loss is heaven's profound gain.

Go rest high, Ashley.

6/24/16

My Little Sissy

Let each generation tell its children of your mighty acts; let them proclaim your power. I will meditate on your majestic glorious splendor and your wonderful miracles.

PSALM 145:4-5 NLT

She's five years younger than I, my little sister Debbie. We hated each other growing up. She told on me and got me in trouble, sometimes when I wasn't even guilty, like the time she sprayed the babysitter with the garden hose, then looked her straight in the eye, and pronounced, "Bicki did it!"

During a fierce fight, she scratched my arm and it got infected. I had to get a shot. Mother made me ride her on the back of my bike. One day she got her toes stuck in the spokes, so I went faster, until they bled. I've always felt guilty about that one.

We just tolerated each other until I went away to college. Then, gradually things changed. There were our weddings and the births of our babies. Since then, we have been there for each other. When my son ran away, he went to Debbie's. Her girls confide in me.

We were allies in the difficult times dealing with a mentally and physically disabled mother. When daddy got cancer, we both cared for him. She was always the good one, I the rebel. Yet she has never judged. She loves me with a fierce loyalty, and I love her. We enjoy each other's company. We laugh at the same things; we make dark-humored jokes, or worse, bad puns. We travel together. Some days we do nothing together— my sister, my friend.

Last night, we went to a play with my dear friend, Martha. I was envying Martha for being financially stable. This morning, Martha called to tell me how lucky I am to have such a close relationship with my sister. She does not have that with her sister. So, as I was envying Martha her money, she was envying me my sister. I am so much the richer one.

Daddies

Fathers, do not embitter your children, or they will become discouraged.

COLOSSIANS 3:21 NIV

My daddy, Russ, has been gone 20 years. Still every day I want to drive to the country and drink coffee with him in his little yellow and brown house at his gray formica table. He was my quiet guide, my counselor, my dry-witted friend. He seldom told my sister and me that we could *not* do something, except for the night he forbade us adult siblings to sleep out in the woods.

"You girls can't sleep out in them woods; there's coyotes up there." Rather, he told us the possible outcomes of our foolishness and let us decide for ourselves. If we chose badly, he let us accept the consequences, while re-affirming his love for us. He never said, "I told you so." He didn't need to. By contrast, our neighbor's father took pleasure in teasing and taunting his children until he provoked them to tears of anger and exasperation. Then he would punish them for crying or acting out in frustration. He thought it was all great fun.

Not everyone had Russ for a daddy. Some of you have memories of a daddy like our neighbor—or worse. For you, my heart aches.

But how I thank God for the gift of my daddy. If God made my earthly daddy in his own image, how sweet it will be to meet Him, my heavenly Father, face to face. Truly I have been blessed with the best in both worlds.

Aunt Jessie

Charm is deceptive, and beauty is fleeting; but a woman who fears the LORD is to be praised.

PROVERBS 31:30 NIV

She lived her adult life within a one-mile radius—half a mile to the right to the garment factory, where she worked; half a mile to the left to the Memorial Baptist Church, where she worshipped. When she was a little girl, she escaped the drudgery of her agrarian roots by walking to the one-room Bald Knob School down by Flat Creek, where she drank in words and handfuls of clear water.

Her dream was to win the eighth-grade spelling bee. Her mother, Myrtle, helped her study words every night by the kerosene light. But then came the flu epidemic of 1917. Myrtle caught the flu and succumbed on Christmas Eve. With the loss of her beloved mother, came the loss of her dream.

Her baby brother, Roy, was sent up the road to be raised by neighbors, which was the custom in 1917. Jessie, being the oldest at 12, had to quit school to raise her two-year-old brother, Russell, who was to become my daddy. So she never got to be a child.

She never really got to be an adult either. Granddaddy disapproved of his daughters getting married, so Aunt Jessie never left home. As I remember, she had always seemed content enough—baking, sewing, reading her Bible. Yet she always wore lipstick and shiny brooches and earrings, and perfume. She was proud of her hip-length hair that she braided and wreathed around her head like a halo, which she deserved.

Jessie lived with granddaddy in a white clapboard house with a brick-walled front porch. She planted pink holly hocks and blue hydrangeas.

She sat outside on the swing in the stifling heat, waving her church fan with the picture of Jesus on one side and the local funeral home on the other. When Debbie and I visited, she made us orange Kool-Aid.

Living through the Great Depression, she had learned to salvage everything, including stout coffee, percolated on the stove, and stored in Mason jars for days. Her homemade blackberry jam helped soften the week-old biscuits. She kept a button box under her bed. She would retrieve it, and teach us to thread a needle with our favorite color thread and sew the buttons onto quilt scraps.

Some days, she let us play in the mysterious attic, where boxes and scary things covered in sheets were stored. At Christmas, she gave us a piece of Juicy Fruit, wrapped in a dollar bill. Daddy taught us to be polite, and say, "Thank you."

In 1964, I won the seventh-grade spelling bee at Bridgeport School. She was just as proud of me, as if she had won it herself. I felt a little sad, because I knew badly she had wanted to win that spelling bee so long ago. That day, she gave me five dollars!

Daddy loved her like the mother that she was to him. She loved us like the grandkids she never had. We were her "dandies." One day, she began to cough up blood. The doctor said it was lung cancer. That was so unfair, because she never smoked.

When she died in 1986, she left behind only her 50-year church pin, a few brooches, and some photos in a crumbling black-paged album tied together with a shoelace. One afternoon, I was at the kitchen table, flipping gingerly through the tattered pages. If the light had not reflected just a certain way, I would never have noticed it. Written in pencil next to a picture of a dapper young man leaning against a gate was, "My dearest Charlie."

Another page showed them standing together smiling, she in a loose-fitting handkerchief dress, he in jodhpurs. In the margin, she had penciled, "Happier times." The last entry I could make out read, "April 14, 1941, Monday. All alone again." I felt like crying.

Later, when I showed the book to Debbie, she pointed out that Aunt Jessie had not always been content. In one picture after the Charlie times, she was scowling and had her hands placed sternly on her hips. In some later pictures, her eyes looked dead. Then gradually there was a transformation until her face had softened in to a sweet serenity. At some point, she had totally surrendered to granddaddy and Jesus Christ. And I wondered, did she give up on Charlie, or did Charlie give up on her? Did he marry another girl? Did he carry a faded picture of Jessie? Did he go to war? Did he die?

And I wish they could have stayed together.

I wish she had surrendered to Charlie too.

Grandma Easterly

A wife of noble character who can find? She is worth far more than rubies. Her husband has full confidence in her and lacks nothing of value.

PROVERBS 31:10-11 NIV

In our family, we coined the word "Dee." It means someone who is precious and cuddly.

She was 4'10" and surrounded by six tall men, one her overbearing husband, Edgar, and five her rambunctious sons. She was full of love and good cheer. She had completed two years of college, a rarity for a woman in the 1930s, but she never worked or even got a driver's license.

She always greeted us warmly and offered her brand of hospitality. Thrifty from living through the Depression, she often offered us food that was well past the expiration date. In fact, in 1969, she served up a casserole made with hamburger that had been in her freezer since 1949, the year of my birth!

Green cheese was frequently on the menu. "Do you like it?" she would happily ask her grandsons. They dutifully stated they did. "Then I will fix you some more!" she happily volunteered. Perhaps the worst was the peanut butter meatloaf—a recipe she had found in her Frugal Family cookbook. We just could not tell her that was good, for fear she might "fix us some more."

She saw light in every situation. Accustomed to listening to six guys at a time, she had learned to tune them out. One day, a tragedy struck in the lives of my eight and 12-year-old sons. Their beloved gerbil died. Expecting sympathy, they told her of its demise.

"That's wonderful!" was her reply.

"But, Grandma, our gerbil died."

"Isn't that wonderful?" she responded a second time. She had tuned them out too. They realized they would get no sympathy, but at least she was always in a good mood.

Even as her health failed, even as her husband of 56 years developed Alzheimer's and died, she remained of good spirit. Her last years were spent alone in the house she had shared with her Edgar and her boys. Even as her world narrowed and she was filled with pain, she was staunch in her love of God and the promise of seeing God and Edgar in heaven. So, until the day she died, she smiled and loved and fully had her being. She was a "Dee."

What Debt?

A friend loves at all times, and a brother is born in adversity.

PROVERBS 17:17 NIV

He was a beloved sports figure in this town; he was a 6'5" 300 lb. monster behind closed doors.

He had promised to care for me and talked me into selling my successful business. As a result, the only income I had was a portion of what my successor made each month as payment on her loan. Some months it was $1,000, some months $600, never nearly enough to pay my living expenses.

The situation had thrown me into a state of anxiety and hopelessness, so much so that I almost forgot the blessing of friends. Ellie, my best friend for 30 years, promised to send me her tithe each month. I objected, but she sent it faithfully every month until my season of desolation was over.

Ten years later, I mentioned to her how she had literally saved my life by sending me her tithe check all those months. But Ellie had forgotten. "What tithes?" she puzzled. She had kept no record, expected nothing in return, and truly had no memory of her loving generosity. I was reminded of the song by Morgan Cryar called, "What Sin?" With friends like Ellie, the enemy can't prevail. "What debt?" What debt indeed!

Friends

Let the word of Christ dwell in you richly as you teach and admonish one another with all wisdom, and as you sing psalms, hymns and spiritual songs with gratitude in your hearts to God. And whatever you do, whether in word or deed, do it all in the name of the Lord Jesus, giving thanks to God the Father through him.

COLOSSIANS 3:15–17 NIV

The long winter days had been cold and gray, like my mood. Then it started snowing— again. Even the weatherman lamented, "It's spring, so what happened?!"

Spring is the hope of things to come, but it wasn't coming that day. I slumped into my cushy beige couch, sluggish and melancholy. As I read my Bible, God reminded me that even though it was cold and dark outside, inside my soul I had a choice. I picked up the phone and called my friends, Camille and Martha. "Let's have impromptu lunch!" I suggested cheerfully. Both of my dear friends admitted that they, too, were feeling down. So we got up!

Outside, the cold air felt invigorating on our faces. Inside the Italian restaurant, the temperature was toasty and it smelled of oregano, basil, and garlic. We ordered spaghetti and a salad. Lunch hour turned into two hours, as we prayed, shared our tales of woe, our happy memories, and laughed at our own foibles.

I silently thanked God for these beautiful women in my life. Then God prompted me, "No, say it to them." So I did. Just then the sun came out! We hugged as we were leaving, each of us feeling warmer, brighter, and basking in the love of Christian friends.

Carolyn

I have brought you glory on earth by finishing the work you gave me to do. And now, Father, glorify me in your presence with the glory I had with you before the world began.

John 17:4-5 NIV

She got up Monday morning and died. She told her son she couldn't breathe. By the time the ambulance arrived, she had gone to live in Heaven, where she surely belongs. Hers was a hard life. She lost her arm in a car accident when she was 19. She survived breast cancer, and the recent death of her younger son. She escaped an abuser, and raised her children on her own. And their children. And their children.

At 73, she was still raising children. She had custody of her 13-year-old great grandson, and was doing a fantastic job. She prepared taxes and worked in the school cafeteria to earn money for him to go the Christian Academy. Carolyn was a true quiet, behind- the-scenes Christian. She attended every spiritual retreat she could afford. She was an active member of the Buck Run Baptist Church, where she volunteered many hours in their clothes closet.

She prayed without ceasing; she glorified His name. She was a young 73, and she lived, really lived, until she died. Our lunch group was blessed to have her, and we will miss her. Rest in peace seems such a trite thing to say, but if anyone ever deserved rest, it is Carolyn. So, rest in peace, Carolyn. Rest with God.

The Encourager

An anxious heart weighs a man down, but a kind word cheers him up.

PROVERBS 12:25 NIV

Yesterday was our monthly writers' group. Usually we share dark, serious stories, which are still very much enjoyed. Yesterday, though, I wanted to read a story I had written at a workshop several years earlier.

At the workshop, we had been instructed to write a news story about an event in a fictitious backwoods town called Hilton. I had chosen an account of a barroom brawl and its aftermath, which was loosely based on fact. I thought it was kind of funny, but I hesitated to share it. Fear of rejection is one of our visceral anxieties. What if I read it out loud, and no one laughed or even chuckled? What if I was met with stone-faced silence? I just couldn't risk it.

Then a voice inside me said, "Take the risk." So I did. And they laughed! They even clapped!

This morning, my telephone rang. It was Claudette, calling to tell me personally how much she enjoyed my story and that we needed some humor in our group. She was somewhat apologetic and said she didn't know if I needed encouragement. I sure did! Who doesn't?

She made me feel I could write *War And Peace*, or at least a *Modern Family* episode. Claudette is my friend and encourager. If you have the gift of encouragement, give it to others. I think I'll go now and start my novel.

Trees Of Wisdom

Choose my instruction rather than silver, and knowledge rather than choice gold. For wisdom is far more valuable than rubies. Nothing you desire can compare with her.

Proverbs 8:10-11 NIV

As I was purging papers in preparation for my move, I came across a prayer I had made to God ten years ago. I had completely forgotten that request to put me in the presence of older, wiser people. Sadly, my sister and I only learned sickness, bitterness, and lack of faith from our mother. At the slightest predicament, she would "fold and collapse." She was basically non-functional for many years. Debbie and I had learned how *not* to be, but I longed to be with elders, who could show me how *to* be.

Lately, I have been aware that God has answered my prayer of a decade ago by putting me in the company of older mentors and friends at First United Methodist Church. Cleland just celebrated the big 8-0. I would not have guessed that, because he is active and engaged in life. He led our Stephens Ministry class. Joan is Cleland's support, and demonstrates how a wife should love her husband. Sarah attends every United Methodist Women's conference, I think, in the United States. She has been faithful to the church for many decades. She has been my quiet mentor. Jean is a fellow Stephen Minister, a woman of few words, but great knowledge.

Ann was a greeter the first time I came to First United Methodist Church. She made me feel welcome with her smile. At communion, when I headed back down the center aisle, she discreetly pointed me back to the left. And Paul McNees—he teases me about my ushering anxiety and refuses to let me fail. Betty Isaacs-Smith is a writer and a vicious Scrabble player. Betty is 91 and deals with severe arthritis, but she is sharp and witty.

They have taught me that life is still good, in spite of age and its accompanying health problems. Each of these people has been through trials and sorrows, but they have landed on their feet. They love the Lord and they love people, and it shows in their spirits. And I love these people, who have taught me to love the Lord more. They are my trees of wisdom, and I am blessed that God answered my forgotten prayer.

Jimmie's Joy

God blesses those whose hearts are pure, for they will see God.

MATTHEW 5:8 NLT

Jimmie is my pew buddy on Sunday mornings. He rides to church on the bus from Stewart Home, a loving facility for the intellectually disabled, where he lives in harmony with his friends. He constantly wears a gaping "O" smile, and tells me over and over how much he loves his church, and asks me over and over if I love him. "Of course, I love you, Jimmie, "I answer—over and over.

Today was Easter service. Our talented choir director and his amazing choir and visiting musicians performed exquisitely, the result of weeks of hard work and dedication required to master the difficult pieces. My heart stung and my soul was pierced with joy and sorrow as the Hallelujah Chorus was performed. The congregation stood in silent reverence. But not Jimmie!

I glanced to my side to find Jimmie swaying without inhibition, a joyous smile on his face. He "directed" the choir with wild gesticulations, waving his arms in surprisingly good rhythm, pointing his fingers upward and then wagging them in the direction of the chorus. He knew innately when the crescendo was coming. His arm movements became more frenetic as it approached, until at the very end, he raised his fists and clenched them in jubilant celebration, then gave a "thumbs up" finale for a job well done. He had completed his directing.

Pure joy and satisfaction adorned his sweet face, and he was not afraid to let it shine. What a happy blessing to be beside Jimmie, as he assisted the choir!

Oh, and he can play a mean handbell. And, yes, I do love him.

Miss Vivien C. Moore

Not many of you should become teachers, my brothers, for you know that we who teach will be judged with greater strictness.

James 3:1 NIV

I meant to tell her how greatly she influenced my life with her steely, yet soft-spoken voice, but I got busy. Thirty-six years went by. Then one day I saw her name in the obituaries. Miss Vivien C. Moore.

Vivien was a stout, stern woman—what we used to call an old maid. She taught senior English. I wonder now if she was happy, but a 16-year-old only wondered how she could get the cute guy in the next aisle to notice her. Some teachers had discipline problems and yelled a lot. Not Miss Moore. She never raised her voice, yet even the most recalcitrant student dared not cross her. She demanded, if not excellence, then the best you could do.

I was somewhat of an English nerd. I liked to diagram sentences and read the books she assigned—except for Homer's *The Iliad*. Miss Moore often gave me extra work. Reading and reporting on *The Iliad* was one of those extra assignments. I read it half-heartedly and presented a lackluster report. It was good enough, but certainly not the best I could do. I knew it; she knew it. I still feel a twinge of guilt for failing her on that.

One day she approached me with a grave look on her face, and told me I was in danger of getting a B for the six weeks, as if that were a deadly fate. I was mortified—a B in Miss Moore's class was catastrophic. I buckled down and brought that grade up to an A.

When I graduated, she gave me a book titled *Apples Of Gold*. The inscription read: "To Vicki, as most original — Vivien C. Moore, June 1, 1967." Could this be why she worked me harder and demanded a bit more of me? In her quiet, no-nonsense way, that woman loved me. So, to Miss Vivien C. Moore, I offer a deep, posthumous thank you.

Fifty years later, the book remains one of my prized possessions. I pulled it from the bookshelf today. The spine is torn and the pages are falling out.

From *Apples of Gold*:

"To learn and never be filled, is wisdom:
To teach and never be weary, is love."

I feared her; I respected her; I admired her, and, yes, I loved her too.

Eva's Forgiveness

O Lord, you are so good, so ready to forgive, so full of unfailing love for all who ask for your help.

PSALM 86:5 NLT

In my business, I purge my files six months after finishing a case. Eva's case was only three months past completion, yet I accidentally pushed "delete" and erased her file. "Oh, dear," I thought. "That was unfortunate, but she will probably never know." The next day, who do you think called, and left a message asking to pick up her medical records? Yes, Eva.

I dreaded to call her back. When I did call, I freely admitted my mistake and sincerely apologized. Her response was not one of anger, which I would have expected. Instead, she gently told me, "That's all right. Everybody makes mistakes. It's not a life or death matter. I can get them from my doctor."

Eva acknowledged that I had made a mistake, forgave me on the spot, and forgot my transgression. I was both humbled and forgiven in the same soft sentence. Would my other clients have been so forgiving? Would I?

What a great attitude Eva demonstrated, so Christ-like in its simplicity. As early as Genesis 50:16-21, God tells Joseph to forgive his brothers for far more egregious and purposeful acts, and Joseph obeys. I thank God for the blessing of Eva, and her quiet reminder to me of God's ultimate forgiveness.

The Space Ship

All praise to God, the Father of our Lord Jesus Christ. God is our merciful Father and the source of all comfort. He comforts us in all our troubles so that we can comfort others. When they are troubled, we will be able to give them the same comfort God has given us.

2 Corinthians 1:3-4 NLT

Kayla had cavities. She needed a filling, a crown, and an extraction. Her insurance dictated that we take her to one of "their" pediatric dentists, David Scaff, about whom we knew nothing. But our fears were unfounded.

All the dental horrors we endured as kids, Dr. Scaff turned into a game. The foreboding dental chair became a spaceship. She enjoyed the ride up and down. He referred to the nitrous oxide as "bubble gum nose." Her gum was numbed with a "big Q-tip." No mention was made at all of the long needle, as he injected her with novocaine. She never saw it, so she never even whimpered.

The drill was his "loud whistle," the filling his "special toothpaste." Best of all, her silver crown was her "own shiny jewel." Then came the extraction. I tried not to wince. He told her he was jiggling her tooth. Out it came without her knowledge, thus without tears! Up she was raised from the spaceship.

Now it was time for the anticipated trip to the toy corner. She chose a big red boinky ball. She was a little surprised at the blood in her mouth, but, again, no big deal was made of it. A few spits and a rinse took care of that.

So, what could have been a terribly frightening experience was transformed into a magical hour in the spaceship. It occurred to me that life is often as we expect it to be. It's about faith and changing our attitudes toward uncomfortable life situations. It's about an earthly, kindly Dr. Scaff, and a tender, loving heavenly Father.

Charlene

All beautiful you are, my darling, there is no flaw in you.

SONG OF SONGS 4:7 NIV

"Oh, how horrible! How tragic!" I thought the first time I saw her. Charlene had no right arm, no left leg, and her back was grossly deformed by scoliosis. She walked uncomfortably with a cane in in her left hand and a prosthetic left leg.

I felt such pity for her. Then, Charlene was placed at our Emmaus table and our discussions began. Pity? No more! Charlene was the most intelligent and creative person at our table. And she was funny! She made horrible one-legged jokes. She was self-deprecating, yet extremely confident.

She had given birth to two children, which she single-handedly raised. (Pardon the pun, but I don't think she would mind.) She was a true Christian.

We didn't know, but she had been selected to be a speech presenter. Her lively speech was peppered with Greek language, difficult concepts, and easy humor. And I realized I no longer saw her less-than-perfect body, but only her beautiful face and countenance.

She could have led a life of bitterness and self-pity, but instead she rose above, thanked God for who she was and the life He had given her.

Would we be so gracious? So full of determination? On days when we struggle or feel sorry for ourselves, let's thank God for our bodies, even though we might have aches and pains, and imagine the sweet face of God's perfect Charlene.

Snuggles

I will be your God throughout your lifetime until your hair is white with age; I made you and I will care for you. I will carry you along and save you.

ISAIAH 46:4 NLT

Rachel came from an abusive marriage. After 25 years of being told she was stupid one too many times, she drew the courage to leave. Stupid? I think not, because she went on to obtain a PhD in music. That was 20 years ago.

Now her children were grown and scattered. She lived alone in her small house, with her music and her church friends to help her pass her days. She settled into singleness and what she described as the "'nothingness' of is this all there is?"

She, like the orchid, was alive, but hardly blooming. She did enjoy her garden, but was having difficulty maintaining it due to a bad back. She decided to hire a yardman. She picked one randomly from the phone book. Mike showed up with mower and garden tools in hand. He did an excellent job, and soon the weeds were gone and the perennials bloomed in harmony at their allotted time.

Speaking of harmony, Mike began to show up when there was no yard work to be done. "Got any chores you need done around the house?" Of course, she found chores for him. In spite of her mistrust, she offered him coffee; he offered to take her out to dinner. He convinced her he was not her past. I guess you know the rest of the story. Yep. At age 69, Rachel married Mike.

She shared her joy with her Emmaus friends. She even told of the happiness of snuggling with a man who cherished her, blushing like a teenager. We teased her by referring to Mike as Snuggles. She giggled and blushed some more. Maybe you are in a lonely season, but don't be surprised if God shakes up your world in a good, most unexpected way. Don't be surprised to wake up and find a manicured lawn and a Snuggles at your door.

Perfect Timing

For everything there is a season, a time for every activity under heaven.

Ecclesiastes 3:1 ESV

Elaine, my Emmaus friend, had been through a bad season. Her mother had been diagnosed with leukemia and died eight months later. Then her husband of 15 years simply decided he was not interested in being married or a father. He left her with three pre-teens to raise alone.

I admired her strength in her adversity. She did get the house. Not wanting to stay there, she rented the upstairs to a nice couple and the basement to a single man. After a year, she decided to put the house up for sale.

The house had been her grandparent's house, which made it all the more important to find a worthy buyer. A sweet young couple with twin babies bought it right away. She found another house and put in an offer. But being Elaine, she worried about what would become of her tenants.

She was to close on her new house on May 1 and take a week's vacation to refinish her floors and get settled. In perfect synchrony, her upstairs tenants found another house and bought it. The downstairs tenant moved into an apartment that suited him better. They both moved out on—May 1.

God took care of them, so she could take care of herself. She got her one week in her new house to prepare for her new life. It all worked in God's perfect timing, so smoothly, so peacefully. And now Elaine lives with her three kids, in her new house with its shiny floors, in a promising new season.

To Be Like Elsie

Light shines in the darkness for the godly. They are generous, compassionate, and righteous.

PSALM 112:4 NLT

Several years ago, I was embroiled in personal problems that had left me feeling hopeless and depressed. I was attending Memorial Baptist Church then, and I usually sat with my friends from Sunday school class, but they were all absent that day. I was sitting alone.

I usually have control of my emotions, but, of course, I picked that day to dissolve into a sobbing, slobbering, heaving heap of humanity. I was so embarrassed! When she saw my despair, a wonderful older woman, named Elsie, slid across the pew, put her arm around me, and gently guided my head onto her ample, comforting bosom. She quietly whispered to me, "You are a precious child of God," as she rocked me like a baby. I will never forget Elsie for her compassion.

This morning in church, in spite of the happy tempo of the music, a woman a few pews in front of me started sobbing. She cried all the way through the songs, and after. She was sitting alone. After the service God told me to say something to her. I did not know what, so I touched her shoulder, and simply said, "I saw your sadness this morning and I prayed for you."

I hadn't known how she would react, but her face brightened. She gave me the biggest hug and said, "Thank you so much!" I had no idea who she was, and she had no idea who I was. I have not seen her since. I just know that, because of Elsie, God led me to pay love forward. God gave me a chance to be like Elsie, and that is an awesome honor!

The Face

...The Lord does not look at the things man looks at. Man looks at the outward appearance, but the Lord looks at the heart.

1 Samuel 16:7 NIV

His face was burned off and grafted back on in 100 surgeries. His right ear was missing, replaced by a deep horizontal scar. His left hand, visible from his shirt sleeve, was webbed and gnarled; his right arm was gone. He had suffered these grievous injuries when he was hit by an IED in Iraq.

He was terribly scarred, yet last night he walked onto a stage in front of several hundred members of a town hall meeting and several million TV viewers. He did it not to ask for pity or help for himself, but to advocate for better health care for his fellow injured veterans.

He sat face-to-face with Donald Trump, a Presidential candidate at the time, and made his plea. He could have shrunk from the unforgiving lights and the hot stage, but he showed his scars and his heart, a generous, brave, unselfish heart—and a beautiful face in the eyes of God.

Dandelion People

Don't be concerned about the outward beauty of fancy hair-styles, expensive jewelry, or beautiful clothes. You should clothe yourselves instead with the beauty that comes from within, the unfading beauty of a gentle and quiet spirit, which is so precious to God.

1 Peter 3:3-4 NLT

I took Makayla for a walk after a long winter. Looking for flowers, I imagined she would pick crocus or tulips, the best-dressed of spring. Instead, she looked down at the dandelion weeds growing out of the sidewalk. "There are some. They're yellow!" She jumped a few steps further. "There're more!" she announced, gleefully. What we would spray with weed killer, she saw as beautiful.

Do we look at some people like the dandelions we see through our adult eyes—scraggly, frightening, not fitting neatly in the garden of life; or do we see them like the flowers Kayla saw—beautiful, proud and bright, in spite of growing in the most barren surroundings? Like Johnny, my client; Johnny wears fatigues and a "do rag," and combat boots. His dirty hair and beard have grown to his waist. He is extremely intelligent, but Johnny is a victim of mental illness. He rambles, but he probably knows more scripture than you or I; he knows right from wrong.

In spite of his surroundings, Johnny is always in a happy mood. He has a beautiful soul. The more I know him, the more I love his heart. Some might fear seeing Johnny on the street; I greet him with true affection, as he stands alone on the sidewalk—a dandelion among the tulips. And I thank God for dandelions and dandelion people.

Robert Zimmerman

Beautiful words stir my heart. I will recite a lovely poem about the king, for my tongue is like the pen of a skillful poet.

PSALM 45:1 NLT

Robert Allen Zimmerman was born on May 24, 1941 in Duluth, Minnesota. Soon his parents moved the family to Texas. From a young age, he was described as inscrutable and unpredictable. When he was 20, he moved to New York City.

A musician, he amassed a small following there, and soon secured a record deal. In 1965, he had his first major hit. That same year, he crashed his motorcycle, sustaining a head injury, resulting in amnesia and slight paralysis. While recuperating, he changed from folk to rock music, and was booed roundly.

He had an affair with a famous folk singer. In 1970, he was widely criticized, but by the mid-70s he earned an honorary doctorate in music from Princeton. In 1979, he became a born-again Christian, only to repudiate Christianity in 1982. He was snubbed at Woodstock, but made a triumphant return at Woodstock II in 1994. He performed for Pope John Paul II.

In an eerie coincidence, he released an apocalyptic album on September 11, 2001. On October 31, 2016, Robert was awarded the Nobel Prize for Literature for "having created new poetic expression within the great American song tradition." He was 75.

He was the first musician to ever win this prestigious award, which was described as the most radical choice in its 115 year history. Not bad for an average-looking, nasal-twanging, lower middle-class boy from Texas. Yet he didn't bother to show up to accept his award. Inscrutable, maddeningly so; genius, beyond measure. For all his ups and downs, this world is the richer for having—Mr. Bob Dylan.

San Bernardino Massacre

You meant evil against me, but God meant it for good in order to bring about the present result, to preserve many people alive.

Genesis 45:5 NASB

San Bernardino, 12/2/15. You know the story. This time, 14 were killed, 22 injured by a radical Islamist couple. This one was all the more disgusting because they killed their co-workers, who had recently given them a baby shower. Yet every time we hear of these despicable people performing despicable acts, we hear also of the heroes.

Shannon John was the hero this time. Shannon threw himself on top of a 27-year-old female co-worker, who later said, "I will always remember his left arm wrapped around me, holding me as close as possible next to him behind that chair, and amidst all the chaos, I'll always remember him saying these three words: "I got you."

Shannon died that day, shielding Denise.

Jesus died, shielding us all. "I got you…" To this day, He has continued to say those words over and over. Jesus and Shannon; Shannon and Jesus—one and the same that day? Shannon is now with Jesus in the glorious realm forever. Glory be!

Facebook Stories

Diagnosis: *Unknown*

Facebook post by Heather Luscher Baggett, used with permission

> *If you remain in me and my words remain in you, ask whatever you wish, and it will be done for you.*
>
> John 15:7 NIV

Last Saturday, we welcomed the last member of our family into the world. It was long and painful and worth every minute. On Monday, an hour before we were to leave the hospital, a pediatrician visited us. He told us that Hazel, our perfect little girl, had weak muscle tone that might be nothing, but might be signs of a serious genetic issue. He referred us to a specialist for testing, then he just walked out! He left his patient with the most painful diagnosis—the *Unknown*.

The next few days, many prayers and tears were offered up for her. My husband did research on genetic disorders associated with the term "floppy baby" and then made me promise not to do the same, but I knew from his reaction that such a diagnosis would affect our daughter her entire life. On Wednesday, we took her for her normal follow-up appointment with our pediatrician.

Our first words to her were regarding the possible diagnosis. She took one look at baby Hazel and said, without a doubt, our child was *not* floppy. She had weak muscle tone, yes, and as a result we were going to have to work harder to get her to eat. She was losing weight so quickly, because she didn't have the muscle strength to suck. The doctor told us that by two months old, she would have outgrown much of this. There was nothing wrong with her!

Of course, my first reaction was to break down into tears of relief in the office; and as we walked out, our hearts were praising God for the healing. It would be easy to say she was just misdiagnosed, that there never was anything wrong with her. But I was reminded that sometimes, while our hearts long for answers, God leaves us in the *Unknown*.

With a definitive diagnosis, we could form a plan, start figuring out how we would adjust our lives and hers to give her the best life possible, but when left with the *Unknown*, we were forced to our knees, knowing that there was nothing for us to do but lay this before God. We are ever reminded of our own helplessness, and His strength and mercy. My daughter was healed by a loving God. This I know.

Another Day

By Peggy Bryant, with permission

Give thanks in all circumstances; for this is God's will for you in Christ Jesus.

1 Thessalonians 5:18 NIV

I was going to gripe about waking up at 2:30 a.m., but instead...
I am thankful to wake up on my own, another day with the gift of life.
Another day to hold loved ones close.
Another day to fight whatever battles come my way.
Another day to enjoy and appreciate the freedoms provided us by the sacrifices made by others.
Another day to be thankful for a job I enjoy.
Another day to do the simple things that I often take for granted.
Another day.
Thank you, Lord!

A Husband's Love

By Kathy Hensley, with permission

> *For husbands, this means love your wives, just as Christ loved the Church... In the same way, husbands ought to love their wives as they love their own bodies.*
>
> EPHESIANS 6:25-28 NLT

The Lord acts in mysterious ways... I was thinking of a few things this morning which are pretty heavy on my heart, and I got a phone call. Oh, it didn't wipe away what I am waiting on the Lord for, but it made my day brighter. My loving husband called and I thought, "Well, he must have forgotten something." Instead he said, "Hold on and listen to this," putting the phone to the radio, playing a love song. I say this to reinforce that love conquers all. The simplest acts of kindness and love you can show could make the biggest difference in someone's life.

All Who Give, For All Who Gave

By Sara Garner, 5/27/16, with permission

So Joshua took control of the entire land, just as the Lord had instructed Moses. He gave it to the people of Israel as their special possession, dividing the land among the tribes. So the land finally had rest from war.

Joshua 11:23 NLT

Today I had the privilege of walking the Frankfort Cemetery and helping find the graves of veterans to make sure they had an American flag placed by their grave. Mr. Butch Graves, himself a vet, has spent weeks placing flags in this and surrounding cemeteries. He's made numerous trips to ensure no one was skipped.

We also watched him as he was getting ready to get back in his truck to remove his hat and stand in silence as "Taps" was played for Mr. Fred Bradley's service. I marvel at the amount of respect previous generations have for our country and her fallen men and women in arms. So often today, people can't stand still or be quiet during the playing of our National Anthem. Please take time to remember, respect, and revere your loved ones and those who paid the ultimate sacrifice for our freedoms this Memorial Day.

I want to thank my dear, sweet friend, Marta Roberts, for also participating in placing flags yesterday. She is a tireless and fierce advocate of our veterans. There are many others who gave their time in this and many projects to honor the memories of our heroic loved ones. To all of you, thank you and may God bless you richly.

And to the veteran I love the most, I thank God for bringing you back from your dangerous deployments from Desert Storm through Iraq and Afghanistan. I love you, Chad Easterly.

Mom

As A Woman Thinketh...

By Jeannie Heltzel Jones, with permission

Give thanks in all circumstances; for this is God's will for you in Jesus Christ.

1 Thessalonians 5:13 NIV

1. Early wake-up = Children to love
2. House to clean = Safe place to live
3. Laundry = Clothes to wear
4. Dishes to wash = Food to eat
5. Crumbs under the table = Family meals
6. Grocery shopping = Money to buy food
7. Toilets to clean = Indoor plumbing
8. Lots of noise = People in my life
9. Endless questions about homework = Kids' growing brains
10. Sore and tired at bedtime = I'm alive!

Daddy's Gift

By Ellen Downey, with permission

Jesus said, "You are blessed, Simon son of John, because my Father in heaven has revealed this to you. You did not learn this from any human being."

Matthew 16:17 NLT

I sure miss my daddy. Today is his 96th birthday. One of his favorite things was going to Cracker Barrel and having the Uncle Herschel's breakfast. So that's exactly what I did today, along with my family.

My brother and sister-in-law did the same in Florida. When we placed our order in Kentucky, the server came back with a card to say our meal was paid! What a surprise and a kind gesture. The benefactor was anonymous. But in my mind, I know it was my daddy saying, "Thanks for thinking of me in such a special way." And what a neat day for all of us to celebrate such a wonderful man.

Thanks, Daddy.

From Facebook Today

Contributor unknown

Praise be to the name of God for ever and ever; wisdom and power are his.

DANIEL 2:20 NIV

Today I woke up. Some people did not. I can see. I can talk. I can hear. I can move. I have hope. I am thankful. With all my heartI give You all thePRAISE!

Great Marriages

Give honor to marriage, and remain faithful to one another in marriage.

HEBREWS 13:4 NLT

As June is a month for many weddings, I copied this short, but profound reminder of what a great marriage should be. It was offered on Facebook by Dave Willis.org.

Great marriages don't happen by luck or by accident. They are the result of a consistent investment of:

Time
Thoughtfulness
Forgiveness
Affection
Prayer
Mutual Respect, and a
Rock Solid Commitment between a husband and wife.

Mondays And Dogs

Contributor unknown

Give thanks to the Lord, for he is good! His faithful love endures forever.

Psalm 107:1 NLT

Woke up feeling kind of upset that it's Monday and I have to go to work… then remembered that some people won't wake up today, and many don't have a job to go to, and some woke up cold and homeless—and some don't even have a dog. Thank you, Lord, for all I have to be thankful for. Have a blessed day, everyone!!

What Goes Around...

Contributor unknown

So in everything, do to others what you would have them do to you, for this sums up the Law and the Prophets.

MATTHEW 7:12 NIV

In 1981, a pediatrician saved the life of a 3 lb., 2 oz. premature baby boy by working around the clock and beating the odds to stabilize him. In 2011, the same pediatrician was pinned inside a burning vehicle after a car crash. He was saved by a young paramedic. That paramedic turned out to be the premature baby he had saved 30 years earlier.

No Wings

Contributor unknown

Are not all angels ministering spirits sent to serve those who will inherit salvation?

HEBREWS 1:14 NIV

A police officer responds to a fire in 1998. He takes a 5 year-old girl, unresponsive, not breathing, from a fireman. The cop does CPR in the back of a patrol car, as his partner races to the hospital. He gets her breathing again just as they arrive at the ER.

In 2016, that same officer attends a young girl's joyous college graduation—the same girl he saved 18 years earlier. By the way, she graduated magna cum laude, with highest honors.

Stress Relief

By Kari Williams, with permission from Jackson

From the lips of children and infants you have ordained praise...

Psalm 8:2 NIV

My awesome son, Jackson, gave me this pep talk when I talked about how I feel stress. (This is the *Reader's Digest* condensed version.)

Jackson: Every day, you go and take people's stress away. They have stress. You hold it in this box in your heart and they feel better. Think how awesome that is. You do this every day for 50, or 25 years and that is so cool. You have to give some of that stress to someone else, like God, or else you will be filled up with it and won't have room for anyone else's stress. That is your job, and that is what you are good at. That's what makes it amazing.

Miscellaneous Miracles

A True God Happening

By Jennifer Reynolds

The right word at the right time is like a custom-made piece of jewelry.

PROVERBS 25:11 MSG

Several years ago I was having lunch at a local Kentucky Fried Chicken restaurant. I was wearing a Christian t-shirt with these words from Psalm 46 printed on the back: "God is our refuge and strength, an ever-present help in trouble. Therefore, we will not fear." A man who was a stranger to me walked up to me and said, "I want to thank you for wearing that t-shirt today. You have helped me more than you will ever know."

I get goose-bumps every time I think of this. God arranged for us to be in the same place at the same time. He knew this man needed to be reminded that God will never leave us, nor forsake us. You just never know how God will work in our lives. We truly serve an awesome God!

The Angel

For He will command His angels, concerning you, to guard you in all your ways; they will lift you up in their hands...

Psalm 91:11-12 NIV

I was five. I had just had my tonsils removed, then I contracted scarlet fever and German measles. I remember feeling so hot and sweating profusely. Mother let me stay in her maple bed, so she could keep a close eye on me, and wipe my brow with a cool cloth.

I remember piling up on her fluffy pillows, and the smell of the lavender sachet on the quilt. I remember the pink satin curtains, blowing in the wind toward my skinny body. I don't remember the angel.

As my temperature rose to 105 degrees, mother said I blissfully announced, "Mommy, look at the beautiful angel!" A hallucination? Delirium? Maybe.

Mother said she was terrified of the angel, thinking it had come to fetch me, to lift me up in her hands. Maybe that angel was just watching over me, protecting me, blowing the cooling wind over my face to lower my fever.

Whatever the purpose of the angel, it could have only been for good. If it was to lift me away, like the Israelites fleeing Egypt, how glorious! ("See, I am sending an angel before you to protect you on your journey and lead you safely to the place I have prepared for you." Exodus 23:2.) If it was to heal me, the angel was my nurse.

Soon my fever broke, and gradually I improved. I believe the angel was there. I believe she was beautiful. I still don't remember her. I wish I did.

Nik-L-Nips

My guilt has overwhelmed me like a burden too heavy to bear.

Psalm 38:4 NIV

If you're old enough, you remember them. Nik-L-Nips, those little cardboard cartons of bottle-shaped paraffin, filled with colored sugary liquid. I liked to bite the tops off, suck out the liquid, then chew the paraffin.

I really liked Nik-L-Nips, especially when I was six. Our next door neighbor, Mrs. Sergent, was a teacher. She often invited us kids over to play in her basement den. Her door was always open, and we were always welcome there.

One summer day, I crossed my yard and went into her den. There was no one there. On her coffee table was a carton of Nik-L-Nips. I wanted those Nik-L-Nips! What to do? No one would see, no one would ever know.

I edged over to the coffee table, where I could pick them up, but instead of excitement, something inside me felt sad. What was it? Still, with a quick glance around, I grabbed those Nik-L-Nips and ran back home, where I hid them under my pillow.

After dinner, I did bite the tops off, suck out the liquid, and chew the paraffin, but they didn't taste as good as I remembered. The paraffin seemed to grow inside my mouth till I spit it all out. There was that sad feeling again, that need-to-cry feeling. Edgar Allan Poe would have called it his tell-tale heart, but my 6-year-old language skills weren't so developed. I just knew I felt sick inside.

All week I didn't sleep well. Then came Friday, allowance day. Daddy gave me my quarter, which I usually spent at the dime store downtown, but this allowance day, I left my quarter at home. The next morning, with the quarter clenched tightly in my fist, I walked over to Mrs. Sergent's den.

I knocked. No one was home. I opened the door, walked quickly to the coffee table, laid down my quarter, then ran out the screen door and back to my room, crying. The tears were not for the relinquished quarter, but for the relief I felt at restitution for the Nik-L-Nips.

Soon the sad feeling in my heart was gone, and my tummy felt better. I didn't know that what I suffered had a name. I just knew mommy and daddy had taught me not to steal, and I had stolen—but I had made amends.

I'm quite sure Mrs. Sergent knew who the culprit was, but she never mentioned the missing Nik-L-Nips or the mysteriously-appearing quarter to me. Funny though, the next time I visited, she gave me a big hug—and a carton of Nik-L-Nips.

Press On

Oh, that we might know the Lord! Let us press on to know Him. He will respond to us as surely as the arrival of the dawn, or the coming of rains in early spring.

Hosea 6:3 NLT

On hot summer days, my mother stood at the wooden ironing board in our knotty pine kitchen. The heated iron caused beads of sweat to fall from her hairline, down to her eyebrows, and onto the board. In her day, there were no steam irons. She used a green Coke bottle filled with water and topped with a cork into which holes had been punched.

She would press our garments, then sprinkle them with the Coke bottle, and press again. Her arm moved in swift, fluid strokes, controlling the sizzle, so as not to hold the iron in one spot too long and leave an iron-shaped burn mark. She stood all day, pressed, sprinkled, and wiped her brow.

Each pressed garment was hung perfectly on a metal rack, then transferred to our closets. When she was finished, her back hurt, but she felt satisfaction as she moved to the kitchen table to sit and cool off with a glass of sweet iced tea. She could have given up, but she persevered all day, literally pressing on until her tedious chore was done.

Some of our days are tedious and tiring, our seasons hot and dry, but we can rest assured that God knows us, and we can seek rest in His arms, waiting for the daylight, waiting for the spring. So press on. Things will iron out.

The Advocate

But the Advocate, the Holy Spirit, whom the Father will send in my name, will teach you all things and will remind you of everything I have said to you.

John 14:26 NLT

Ad-vo-cate (noun) l. a person who publicly supports or recommends a particular cause. (verb) 2. to publicly support, to champion, to speak on behalf of, to argue for, to lobby for

On 2/15/94, after much prayer and even some prophetic dreams, I opened my own business. I named it Kentucky Disability Advocates. My mission was to walk Social Security disability clients through the labyrinthine bureaucracy and represent them before administrative law judges. The paperwork, rules and regulations I knew from adjudicating claims for state government for 20 years. The advocate part was up to me to define.

Immediately, I noticed my clients came to me ready to give up, feeling that no one would listen to them. Right away, I decided to look at each face that came in as a person, not just as a blue folder. As they became familiar with me, they shared their lives, their families, their birthdays, their tragedies. The more we knew each other, the easier it was for me to advocate for them.

I prayed for God to ease their burdens. Before each hearing, I prayed, not just to win, (though admittedly that was part), but to do a respectable, knowledgeable job of speaking on their behalf. Most cases we won; still my prayers and preparation did not earn me a 100 percent win rate.

God knows us. He sees our faces. He will listen to us and intercede on our behalf. But we must first try to know, really know Him.

Pretend He is sitting face-to-face with you. What will you say to Him? Tell Him your worries, your triumphs and tragedies. He already knows them anyway. Then pick up a Bible. Ask God to help you understand what He is saying to you. Spend time with Christian friends, who can explain how great is your God. Plead your case.

God never loses; he has a 100 percent win rate for you. I tried to be filled with the Holy Spirit as I went about my work as an advocate. God *is* the Holy Spirit! He will never fail you. He will support you, champion your cause, be your spokesman when you cannot find the words. God is It. He is the ultimate Advocate. Be reminded of this always.

The Ant

Go to the ant, you sluggard; consider its ways and be wise. Though they have no prince, or governor, or ruler to make them work, they labor hard all summer, gathering food for the winter.

PROVERBS 6:6-9 NLT

Last summer, our town was plagued with ants—big ants. One morning, I sluggishly stumbled into the bathroom and flipped on the light switch. The ants swarmed.

One, in particular, was crawling around the sink drain. Annoyed, I turned on the water full blast. The ant clung mightily to the drain, before being swept away. Good riddance, I thought. Then, to my surprise, the ant reappeared. With great tenacity, it had climbed out of its torrent of impossibility. I must admit I respected that ant.

How many of us would cling so fiercely in the middle of a swirling storm? Would we give up and be churned into a watery abyss? An ant brain has 250,000 brain cells, compared to a human with 10 million, yet that ant was wise enough and strong enough to fight for its survival.

Surviving the storms of life takes strength and wisdom. Even with our 10 million brain cells, we cannot do it alone. Unlike the ant, we have a Prince and Ruler. We need the strength and wisdom that comes from knowing God's plan for our lives. Remember the ant in your next tempest. Cry to God, your Savior, cling tightly to His mighty hand, then trust that He will pull you up and rescue you.

The Art Show

He has made everything beautiful in its time. He has also set eternity in the hearts of men; yet they cannot fathom what God has done from beginning to end.

ECCLESIASTES 3:11 NIV

All autumn I had awakened early, so I could sit in the dark with my coffee and watch as the giant oak tree outside my living room window came alive with a burst of orange and gold. Then I would turn my eyes to my Bible, and spend time in the early morning light reading scripture and talking to God.

This morning, though, I slept in. When I opened the shutters, the sky behind my tree was already swirled by God's spatula into peaks and strands of fuchsia. I felt a warm joy at the sight.

"I'll go get my coffee and come sit and enjoy it," I thought on my way to the kitchen. But when I got back, the fuchsia whirls had settled behind the hills. I had missed the show; the curtain call had come too soon.

That is the way when we turn our eyes form God, just for a minute. The light disappears. The strong tree of life still stands, and the light will come again in the morning, but we have missed a moment of glorious beauty we could have shared in communion with our heavenly Father. So wake up in time to see His breathtaking art exhibit. Your coffee can wait.

For the beauty of the earth, for the glory of the skies, for the love which from our birth, over and around us lies. Lord of all to thee we raise this our hymn of grateful praise.

Words by F.S. Pierpoint, 1864; Music by C. Kocher, 1838

The Atheist

One day as Jesus was walking along the shore of the sea of Galilee, He saw two brothers— Simon, also called Peter, and Andrew, throwing a net into the water, for they fished for a living. Jesus called out to them. "Come follow me, and I will show you how to fish for people!" And they left their nets at once and followed him.

MATTHEW 4:18-20 NLT

I belong to a community theatre group. We're a pretty tame group of thespians, except for Dan, who is an avowed atheist. I have heard some vile utterances from his mouth—and not on stage.

I pray for him, but I have tried to steer clear of any conversations about Christianity. Last week, Dan lost a dear friend. He issued a Facebook eulogy to honor her. To my surprise, the thing he remembered and admired most about her was her talks to him about Christ and salvation. He admitted that he had given her a hard time when she spoke of God, but she had gently persisted—and he had listened. He had heard! Her words had pierced his unbelieving heart.

His words pierced my soul. I was ashamed. Yes, I prayed for Dan, but I had a spirit of timidity. It is easy to "preach to the choir"; it's to the non-believers I must speak up and let my faith be known. What if Jesus had walked on by when He saw Simon and Andrew fishing? What if He had remained silent, as I had? Never again will I hold my tongue if I can reach a doubter. Forgive me, Jesus. I'm going out fishing now.

A Bottle Of Sorrows

You keep track of all my sorrows. You have collected all my tears in your bottle. You have recorded each one in your book.

Psalm 56:8 NLT

Ever spill a bottle of water, just one single bottle? It seems like so much more comes out than what went in. How can a small bottle, when spilled, cover a table, the dishes, the floor, the walls, and even splatter into the next room?

Yet ponder the infinite number of tears shed by humanity since time began. We have all cried tears throughout our lives, sometimes just a few at a time; other times copious, tissue-filling tears; sometimes the silent, dry tears of our souls. They mount up. We cry and forget. We cry and He remembers. He remembers our sorrows and sends His soothing showers of comfort.

What a heavenly store of tears He keeps in His endless reservoir! I like to think He releases them just enough at a time to dry someone's tears, while making room for the one whose tears are next. When our own tears have dried, we can use the remembrance of our sorrows to wipe the eyes of the newly heartbroken.

All our weepings are saved in His clouds of love for us, to be stored or released as our lives ebb and flow. So if you are in a season of despair, look to the heavens. There you will find God's measure of mercy opened to your name, your tears collecting, until your sorrow has passed, and your tears become healing rain.

The Breakdown

The Lord is gracious and compassionate, slow to anger and rich in love. The Lord is good to all; he has compassion on all he has made.

Psalm 145:8-9 NIV

Chad's friend, Clay, was a wild teen, ready to fight the world. The product of an absent father and a mentally disabled, yet loving mother, he was angry. Toughness was the way he handled his feelings of pain and rejection. He had, in fact, met my son when they challenged each other to a street fight. When it became a draw, they gained a healthy respect for each other, and the friendship was born.

One Sunday, while driving alone on Georgetown Road, Clay's old Chevy truck broke down—directly in front of the Buck Run Baptist Church. It was 11:05 a.m. He looked around for someone to help him, but all the church members were in the morning worship service. He had no phone (this was before cell phones), so no way to call for help. It was winter. Discouraged and cold, he decided to go inside. He quietly found a pew. After the service, he was greeted with love by that Godly congregation. There, he found physical and spiritual warmth that day.

Today, Clay is still a member of Buck Run Baptist Church. So, too, are his wife and five children. Truly there was blessing in the breakdown. His life was re-started by a truck that wouldn't.

The Camels

By Debbie Smith

For all the animals of the forest are mine, and I own the cattle on a thousand hills.

Psalm 50:10 NLT (Camels, too!)

I knew there were camels in Arizona. Just before I visited my daughter who lived there, I had read a book that said there were. One might possibly see descendants of camels that had once been raised for military duties before the Civil War and then were abandoned to the deserts of southwest Arizona, a little-known historical fact.

I began to pray on my trip to my daughter's home. "Please, Lord, it would be so exciting to see a camel traipsing across the barren terrain on one of our road trips, and I know you can make it happen, Lord! Please!"

We did visit the desert and the amazing Sedona formations; still there was no camel to be seen. We spent the day before departure home caring for a friend's baby. She had a beautiful home, complete with a pool and lush landscaping, but my thoughts were still on the fact that the chances of spying a free-roaming camel were over. Not Even One Hump!

Toward the afternoon, my two daughters and I brought the baby inside and began straightening the house. I had kitchen duty. I shuffled items around as I wiped the counter tops—and stopped dead in my swipe! Leaning against the backsplash was a small decorative picture of not one, but two camels! Not roaming the desert, but camels nonetheless. Touche, Lord, Touche!

A Cup Of Starbucks

Make sure that nobody pays back wrong for wrong, but always try to be kind to each other and to everyone else.

1 Thessalonians 5:15 NIV

We were taking prayer requests in Bible study today. While we asked for relief from suffering and tragedies, Judie Blake spoke up excitedly and said, "I have a blessing!" She was so happy, I thought it would be a cure for someone's terminal illness.

Instead, she told of how she stopped in Starbucks this morning for (what else) coffee. She handed her Starbucks gift card to the cashier, who informed her she only had $1.47 left. Now we all know $1.47 will not buy a cup of Starbucks coffee.

Judie headed back to her car to get the rest of the money, but the cashier stopped her. "Don't go back out in the cold," he said. "I'll cover it today." Judie insisted she had the money. "No, let me get it," the cashier commanded. "Just pay it forward."

After she told her story, she took a sip from her green and white Starbucks coffee cup, and leaned back satisfied. Kindness is never a small blessing. The blessing was increased when each of us agreed to pay our own kindness forward. There were 15 of us there that day. By telling her story, Judie had multiplied one kindness times 15.

A Different Light

For you know it was not with perishable things such as silver and gold that you were redeemed from the empty way of life... But with the precious blood of Christ, a lamb without blemish or defect.

1 Peter 1:18-19 NIV

In the store, it was hard to tell if the shiny earrings were silver or gold. The clerk thought they were silver. I asked a customer, who also felt they were silver. I wanted silver, so I bought them.

When I got home, I excitedly took them out of the tissue. The deceptive ambient lighting in the store had cast a dimmer glow. My living room light was bright and less forgiving. Clearly, they were gold.

I felt some disappointment. Yet the truth was, I didn't really need earrings at all—I just wanted them. The money I had spent for those earrings, which would have dangled uselessly from my ears, was enough to buy a meal for a needy family. I carefully re-wrapped them in the tissue, and returned them to the store, where the clerk cheerfully refunded my money.

Then I drove to the soup kitchen and surrendered my refund. The feeling it gave me was worth more than silver or gold. It was downright shiny!

Dump Trucks

Humble yourselves before the Lord, and He will lift you up.

James 4:10 NIV

Cameron is a skinny four-year-old boy with white hair, clear blue eyes, and more than a slight touch of ADHD. His parents were unable to care for him, so his mamaw, my friend, was doing her best to raise him. To give her a few hours of free time, I was keeping Cameron one summer afternoon.

He played contentedly with a big red and yellow dump truck. His truck was loaded with dirt, bug wings, rocks, and to my dismay, some of my gerbera daisies, which he had sprinkled colorfully over his "load." He was in that other world of little boys, pushing the truck back and forth. Vroom!

Then the wheels became stuck in the dirt ridge between the sidewalk and the grass. Cameron was tough. He had a challenge. He tried mightily to move that truck. I stayed out of it, allowing him to try to think of a solution, but ready if he needed me. His determination slowly turned to frustration, as the truck tilted dangerously to the left, threatening to dump his hard-earned cargo.

Finally, on the verge of tears, and admitting he could not free the truck by himself, he cried, "Help me, Bicki!" And so I did. When your life's dump truck is stuck, be assured God is watching and waiting until you humble yourself and cry to Him. Then He will reach down with His mighty hands and right your load, all for the asking, all for your cry of, "Help me, Lord!"

The Dungeon Of Depression

Praise be to the God and Father of our Lord Jesus Christ, the Father of compassion and the God of all comfort, who comforts us in our troubles, so that we can comfort those in any trouble with the comfort we ourselves have received from God.

2 Corinthians 1:3-4 NIV

1985 is a year I will never remember. I spent it in the dark dungeon of depression, dreading to be awake because of the pain that engulfed me. Yet I could not sleep. I could not eat. I became a skeletal 90 pounds.

A mysterious illness of severe pain and fatigue had struck. (It is now known as fibromyalgia.) Then came the break-up of an eight-year relationship. Looking back, I see that the stress of working and raising two little boys alone had also contributed to my great depression.

I begged God to take the pain away. He said, "Not now." In my fog of despondency, I failed to appreciate my mother, who came to live with me and take care of my children; my sister, who has always been there; my friends, who took me out for rides and told me they loved me; my boss, who kindly held my job open; my doctor, who assured me I would recover; my life-saving medications.

Most of all, I thank my Heavenly Father, who kept a close eye of protection on me during that year in the abyss. Gradually, I emerged from the pit of despair. I did recover. Occasionally, a gray fog still covers my being, but it's a good life, and from my brokenness, I can help piece others back together.

The Eagle

Yet those who wait for the Lord will gain new strength. They will mount up with wings like eagles. They will run and not get tired. They will walk and not become weary.

Isaiah 40:31 NIV

The YouTube video showed an eagle in a two-inch deep paint tray of water. There was no explanation of how or why it was there. But clearly this eagle was not where it belonged. It couldn't move. Its head fell and bobbed into the water; the eagle jerked it out in fear, but its face was angry. Its neck was wobbling. The power, but not the determination, was gone from its head.

It flapped its wings wildly to dislodge the water, but its magnificent wings settled impotently back into the tray. Eagles aren't meant to flap; they are meant to soar. There was no room for spreading. It tried to escape by walking, but its legs were scrawny and weak, stumbling over each other.

Was it fear or a physical reason it could not escape? Was it in danger, or did it just need to calm down? The eagle was made to fly in the air; this eagle was in water—the wrong element.

How sad to see this usually intimidating, powerful creature rendered helpless by its circumstance. Are you in a situation you should not be in? Mired in your own paralysis and indecision? Calm down. Stop flapping. Ask God to ease your fears and give you the strength to escape. Maybe you truly are in the deep water of despair, but maybe you're just in a paint tray. Soar away!

A Good Day

Don't look out for your own interests, but take an interest in others, too. You must have the same attitude that Christ Jesus had.

PHILIPPIANS 2:4-5 NIV

I was waiting in my ophthalmologist's office for my cataract surgery. I felt old, cold, hungry, and as if a small rodent was gnawing on my back. Then my phone went dead.

Having nothing to entertain me, I resorted to actually thinking. This caused me to examine my attitude. Yes, I was getting older, but I had made it this far, and I could still half-see. I was cold, so I got my coat and wrapped it snugly around my shoulders. My back hurt, but there was a woman in the waiting room with no legs. I was hungry, but not starving.

My impending bad mood gave way to a big "thank you" to my God for His utter goodness to me. My surgery caused barely any discomfort, and now I had the gift of whole vision again. And about the hunger—we stopped at Cracker Barrel on the way home, where we had meatloaf, homemade mashed potatoes, biscuits with honey, and sweet iced tea. God provided me with money to satisfy my hunger, and the sweet presence of my sister to share it with. Now that's a good day.

The Goodwill Concerto

by Debbie Smith

Myrrh, aloes, and cassia perfume your robes. In ivory palaces the music of strings entertains you.

Psalm 45:8 NLT

It was late afternoon at the local Goodwill thrift store. Browsing there for bargains was a form of stress relief for me, but not so much today! A very old and dilapidated piano in front of the store was a child magnet. Little fingers banged out dissonant notes that bounced from wall to wall. I moved to the back of the store to escape the cacophony, lamenting about the children and parents who no longer disciplined them.

In a few moments, I heard another tentative plink or two on the keys and cringed at what was to come. What came were beautiful, haunting strains of a classical song that wafted through the store, as beautiful as any I had ever heard in a concert hall. Not even the badly out-of-tune piano could disguise the full, melodious sound. Murmurs of surprise and praise rippled through the customers and staff.

I eased toward the front to get a glimpse of the maestro. To my amazement, the prodigy who rose from the bench was a tall, lanky, red-haired young man in his twenties. He was dressed in an old green tee-shirt and dirty, worn-out jeans.

Admiring customers clapped. "Did you have to stop?" the cashier asked. "I could have listened to that all night!" The young man grinned a rather sheepish grin and shuffled over to his girlfriend who was casually looking through a rack of CDs.

The Harvest

And they will see his face, and his name will be written on their foreheads. And there will be no more night there—no need for lamps or sun—for the Lord God will shine on them. And they will reign forever and forever.

Revelation 22:4-5 NLT

Os Hillman, in his book, *The Upside Of Adversity*, mentions "a great end-time harvest of souls." Perhaps we are in end times. Circumstances would lead us to believe so. A recent CNN story told of the Doomsday Clock, which has an internationally recognized design and conveys how close we are to destroying our civilization with "dangerous technologies of our own making," naming nuclear weapons, climate change, and biotechnology, which could "inflict irrevocable harm, by intentions, miscalculation, or accident." Pretty scary stuff, especially when our leaders have their fingers on the nuclear buttons.

It's true that anything man makes, he can use for good or evil. Yet the doomsday countdown involves an arrogance and self-importance mankind has placed on himself. We have been predicting our doom for thousands of years. In doing so, we denigrate God—the maker of us all. He is the ultimate maker of everything. He will decide what hour the end will come.

Doomsday infers horrific catastrophe. It is our choice whether we suffer catastrophe or resplendent, unimaginable eternal bliss on that day. Doomsday or Glory Day. Read today's verse, then you decide where you will harvest your soul.

Could there be a greater miracle?!

The Henderson Settlement School

"They gave out of their wealth; but she, out of her poverty, put in everything—all she had to live on."

Mark 12:44 NIV

The Henderson Settlement School is a helping community deep in the Appalachian Mountains in tiny Frakes, Kentucky. The drive there is through steep, snaking roads. Poverty there is abject. There is a thriving farm on the property, providing cattle, goats, crops, and firewood. It employs local citizens. To keep the community in operation, many people come there to do mission work.

The week I volunteered, we were served delicious meals in the cafeteria by courteous cafeteria workers. They even offered to open early so we could get our coffee. They served humbly and quietly. After our brains awoke, we were given our assignments. Some chose the office, some the library, some the sewing room.

I like shopping and thrift stores, so naturally, I chose to work in the thrift store. There, I witnessed folks from different churches, including my own, come together for the good of the poverty-stricken people of the mountains. God sent the right personalities to mesh and get the job done.

Some of my group worked in the back room, which was piled to the ceiling with donations that needed to be sorted and put out. One lady, who jokingly referred to herself as OCD, was a terrific organizer. Ollie, the creative one, suggested putting outfits together and hanging them on racks, instead of just folding items and putting them out on tables. How much more attractive the store was when we were finished!

At night, after dinner and worship, we were allowed to shop in the gift shop. Selling handcrafted items is one way for people to make money, now that coal mining has all but disappeared. Beautiful carved woodcrafts, intricately stitched blankets, woven shawls, and ornate turquoise jewelry prominently adorned the store—all made by local talented artisans.

However, in one corner, in a little breadbasket, were simple colored necklaces, made with braided thread. Some even had flecks of gold woven in. I imagined a young wife in her trailer with her babies and no job skills, sitting and twisting the thread she could afford into necklace after necklace. She asked only five dollars for each one.

The thought of the necklace girl touched my heart. I bought several of them. I did not need them all, but I did need the blessing that came from helping my unseen sister of the mountains.

The Kiss

by Debbie Smith

His (Elijah's) preaching will turn the hearts of fathers to their children, and the hearts of children to their fathers...

MALACHI 4:6 NIV

I needed cleaning supplies, so I went to a discount store on "that side of town," where I could get them cheaper. This particular store was certainly not one of my favorites. I stood in line with my paper towels and detergents, and became aware that I was wearing a slightly disapproving look on my face.

I sized up those in front of me—especially the young, scruffy-looking man who was holding a toddler wearing only a diaper. The baby looked intently at the man, but absolutely no interaction took place between the two. "Well, what a great life that baby is going to have," I smirked to myself.

Then the baby turned his little face up close to the man's face and pursed his lips. I waited for the rebuff that I was sure would come. But the man looked down and very gently gave the baby a light, tender kiss. No words were spoken between the father and son; none were needed.

Ashamed, I asked God's forgiveness for my judgmental attitude. This time, there was no smirking.

The Line

If you have any encouragement from being united with Christ, if any comfort from his love, if any fellowship with the Spirit, if any tenderness and compassion, then make my joy complete by being like-minded, having the same love, being one in spirit and purpose. Each of you should look not only to your own interests, but also to the interests of others.

PHILIPPIANS 2:1-2, 4 NIV

I often let people in the grocery line go in front of me, if they have just a few items, and I have a cart load. It just makes sense, but I never really gave it much thought. This day in Kmart, however, a girl at the front of the line was arguing about the price of a bean bag pillow and insisted on a price check, which took 15 minutes. Then she haggled about the price of a 12-pack of toilet paper. Really? My back was hurting very badly, and I felt I might have to get out of the store and leave my purchases behind.

I did not offer to let anyone go ahead. But then it happened to me. The customer in front of me offered me her place in line! With gratefulness, I gladly took it. A small act of kindness and consideration, but a huge relief for me. A reminder that there are no small miracles. A reminder to pay it forward.

A Little Yeast

The Kingdom of Heaven is like the yeast a woman used in making bread. Even though she put only a little yeast in three measures of flour, it permeated the whole loaf.

MATTHEW 13:33 NLT

Paul warned the Galatians that when they were on the right track, they might experience confusion from the one who is not of Him. We are a batch of people, each made of different ingredients, each given special gifts, as well as weaknesses. We are like a loaf of bread.

Although yeast is certainly necessary for bread to rise to golden perfection, if it is dissolved in water that is too cool or too hot, in remains dormant and the bread will not rise. Making bread is a confusing process. All of the ingredients are important, but the misuse of this one single ingredient can be the difference between success and failure.

When we are too cold or even too hot in our pursuit of God, we can ruin His whole recipe for our lives. A person from a bad batch can flatten our walk with Christ. Pray for such people, but distance yourself. Use the yeast of your life to rise to the top. There you can see Him more clearly.

Arms And Ears

Surely the arm of the Lord is not too short to save, nor his ear too dull to hear.

Isaiah 59:1 NIV

Perhaps you've seen the unlikely commercial that features an alligator dining at a fancy restaurant with his well-to-do human friends. When it is time to pay the bill, his short arms conveniently can't reach far enough to pick up the ticket, always leaving the annoyed humans to pay the tab. And perhaps you remember, as a child, your mother putting earache drops in your ear, then stuffing in a cotton ball. How was your hearing then—dull, maybe?

As humans, our arms are sometimes long enough to save one person. My friend, Patsy, was pulled back from certain death by her friend, Sally, as she stepped off a New York street curb into the path of a car. If we humans can reach far enough to save one person, there is *no* length that God cannot go to save us all.

Last week, I didn't hear the siren come up behind me in the car. I don't know why. Maybe my Christmas carols were playing too loudly; maybe I was talking to Chris in the passenger seat. Thank God he heard, and that I was able to pull to the side of the road just as the ambulance sped by. That day, Chris's ears saved us and the ambulance patient.

Maybe God moved Sally's arms; maybe God inhabited the ears of my son. We as humans do all we can to help those who need us, but only God can reach His omnipresent arms to rescue all of us, and to hear our cries for help and answer our pleas. He alone is our arms, ears, eyes, and mouth—always poised and ready to save us, no matter what the peril.

As A Man Thinketh...

For as he thinketh in his heart, so is he.

Proverbs 23:7 KJV

Today I was scrolling through the task bar on my computer. Among the usual prompts of "Scan selected files" and "Create a CD", I noticed "Change behavior". I had never seen this, and had no idea what it meant as far as computer tasks. However, since it was a new year, the "Change behavior" prompt seemed to be speaking directly to me, as I had vowed to do just that this coming year.

I took a personal behavior inventory: Treating people nice, check; Obeying laws, check; No cursing, ooh, ½ check; No overeating, no check; No negative thinking, big no check. All these could be easily changed with a little will power.

The one that zinged me most was No negative thinking. Not until the inventory, did I stop to ponder how often and deep-seated negative thoughts can become. "Bet it'll rain all day." "That jerk cut me off in traffic." "Just when my bills get caught up, my car breaks down."

Admittedly, some of my "sky is falling" attitude is inherited, but it is my responsibility to nip it, as Barney Fife used to say. Before we know it, a bad day's attitude can morph into a negative life attitude.

How's your behavior? How's your attitude? Need to change anything? Take inventory now. Take a deep breath, ask God to help you find a right spirit, then push that "Change behavior" button.

As A Mother...

"Can a mother forget the baby at her breast and have no compassion on the child she has borne? Though she may forget, I will not forget you!"

ISAIAH 49:15 NIV

On June 20, I responded to my friend's concerns with this e-mail:

What fears are you dealing with? I will keep praying for you. Last night I had Kayla. We went into the bathroom to get band-aids out of the wall cabinet behind the toilet. When I opened the door, the whole thing came crashing down on my head, and crunched my neck, shattering glass all over the floor. Then it was falling forward onto me. It was heavy, but I had to balance it, so I could get it off me to keep from injuring my back.

Kayla ran out, literally screaming in fear. She cried out for her mother. I couldn't get to her until I got the cabinet off my back, so she had to be terrified and alone until I could reach her. She hugged me tight, and I told her everything was all right. Then she just relaxed in my arms and her fears were alleviated. She had absolute faith in me that things were under control.

So, my point is, God is like that. He will put situations in our path, but give us the strength to endure them. When we do scream and cry out in fear and seek Him, He comes to us. He will run to us, and hold us tight. It reminds me of the fourth verse of the hymn "Praise To The Lord, The Almighty", lyrics by Joaquin Neander, 1680. "Then to thy need, God as a mother doth speed, spreading his wings of grace o'er thee."

Five centuries later, we can describe our God the same way. I had never thought of God as a mother; I found that very comforting. God does know you and loves you and accepts you, just like I love Kayla unconditionally, even when she throws a tantrum. Wonder why it is so hard to love ourselves when the most important being in the universe thinks we're okay? God, our Father *and* Mother.

Attendant Angel

Share each other's burdens, and in this way you will fulfill the law of Christ.

Galatians 6:2 NIV

Our flight from Panama City to Atlanta had just landed, and we were behind schedule. People rushed into the aisle, impatient and fearful of missing their connections. Midway down the plane, an elderly man was having trouble getting his cane from the overhead bin. He had placed it in front of the bin before we took off, but it had shifted to the back during the flight. He tried his best to reach it, but he was weak, and it was futile. He was becoming flustered, as he continued to hold up the line.

Suddenly, the woman behind him jumped right up, stood on the seat below the bin, leaned into the bin practically throwing her whole body in, and retrieved the cane. Smiling at him, she explained that she used to be a flight attendant, and had done that many times.

An ordinary passenger might have been irritated, or felt inappropriate leaping to the man's rescue, but God put that compassionate former flight attendant directly behind the old man on that flight. After seeing that his wife was safely out of her seat first, he opened his cane, and slowly exited the plane—with his attendant angel still vigilant right behind him.

Better A Dry Crust

Better a dry crust with peace and quiet than a house full of feasting, with strife.

PROVERBS 17:1 NIV

I was young. I was in love. I wanted to impress. The way to a man's heart is through his stomach, right? So for my good old boy baseball player, what could win his heart more than apple pie?

I peeled and sliced the apples, added brown sugar, cinnamon, and nutmeg. It smelled like cozy. Then came the crust. Ellie's mother, Georgie, made the best flaky pie crust ever. Using her recipe, I carefully measured the flour, sugar and salt, then cut in the butter until it resembled "coarse meal."

Then, with great struggle, I rolled it out and gently laid it in the pie plate. Finally, I added the apple filling, covered it with the top crust, and crimped the edges. Into the oven it went.

The cinnamon apple aroma filled the kitchen with warmth and my heart with happiness. Soon the pie was done. I smelled perfection! I had made the perfect pie!

Yet, when I took it out, I discovered the top crust had shrunk and was flooded with apple juices. There is a difference between flaky and dry. My pie was proof. That crust was downright concrete. A small tap with a knife sent hard chunks flying.

I was mortified. What was I to do? He would be here in just a few minutes. Before he arrived, I went to my Bible for some comfort—and God led me straight to, yes, Proverbs 17:1! Thank you, Lord!

As soon as he walked in, he commented on the delightful smell. I made a joke about the crust, as I served him up a warm piece of pie. We both laughed. We made comfortable conversation, and there was peace in my kitchen, as we chiseled out our pie. By the twinkle in his eyes, I could tell I had won his heart.

Frozen

All whose hearts were stirred and whose spirits were moved came and brought their sacred offerings to the Lord.

Exodus 35:21 NLT

My strawberry mango smoothie was too thick. Slurp as I might, the stubborn confection refused to move past my cold, aching teeth. What little I could taste was yummy, but I wanted a generous sip.

Then I noticed a straw on the table, left over from last night's iced tea. I picked it up and stuck it into the smoothie and began to stir it. First the edges, then the center of the smoothie softened with help of the swirling straw. After a few minutes, I was able to sip the tasty, melting smoothie.

The stirring of our hearts is the same. Do you, or someone you know, have a frozen heart? Maybe a pain too great to bear has frozen it. It takes time, but with persistent, gentle stirring, your heart can melt and come alive again.

That wall of pain around the edges will soften first, with the love and prayers of what I call "straw people." God and those people will keep stirring and awakening your heart, until later, maybe much later, you will feel the softening of the center, and when the ice has melted from your soul, you will taste again the deliciousness of life.

Let the "straw people" in. Pray, confess, cry, laugh with them – feel the sweet life seeping back in, feel your heart warming again. Then offer God a sacred thank you from the bottom of your soft, slushy heart.

Brass Lamps

For such people are false apostles, deceitful workers, masquerading as apostles of Christ. And no wonder, for Satan himself masquerades as an angel of light. It is not surprising, then, if his servants also masquerade as servants of righteousness. Their end will be what their actions deserve.

2 Corinthians 11:13-15 NIV

E-mail from Ellie in West Virginia, to me, 5/15/16

Today I had a major breakthrough when I threw away my favorite lamp that I found in the attic back in Kentucky. It had nearly caught on fire here, and it was impossible to find anyone here who could repair it. I also threw away the custom-made shade I had bought for it in a little shop in Lexington. The man in the shop said it was a really good lamp, solid brass throughout. He said they don't even make them like that anymore. On newer lamps, some parts are only brass-plated. So it was one of the last good things I had in my house in Kentucky. Good memories. Well, it's in the garbage now. It's OK.

My response, 5/16/16

Regarding clearing things out and being organized, did you read today's *Jesus Calling* devotional? The lamp is indicative of Satan's temptation. It's shiny and real brass, but if it doesn't work and catches on fire, it's of no use, even dangerous. Like everything else, God lets us know when it's time to move on, and He has something better if we just give up the brass lamps of life, even if it's just the satisfaction that we took action. It will get easier for you to let go of things. I'm proud of you.

Busy Friends

Two people are better than one, for they can help each other succeed. If one person falls, the other can reach out and help...

Ecclesiastes 4:9-10 NLT

We usually have lunch on Fridays—Martha, Camille, Judy, and I; but this week Judy had been sick, Camille had to work through lunch, and Martha was busy. Around lunchtime Friday, I visited a sick friend in the hospital. As I was leaving, I ran into Martha coming in to visit another patient. I was happy to see her. Even though we couldn't have lunch, God gave us this serendipitous time to briefly chat.

Martha told me about the week she had had—taking her grandson to baseball and soccer games, and about the praise that her brother had finally found a job after two years of unemployment. I enjoyed our impromptu time together.

Later that afternoon, I received a text from her, apologizing for the "drama" and saying she just needed to vent. What she had seen as boring drama, I had seen as the life of a busy, blessed woman. I immediately texted her back that she was *never* to apologize for venting— that's what friends are for, and that I was thankful for her and all my friends. And, oh, how I am!

But It Doesn't End Here

Hope deferred makes the heart sick, but a dream fulfilled is a tree of life.

PROVERBS 13:12 NLT

Ellie had a bad week. Her fancy fridge went out—for the third time. The store had been discourteous and slow to respond to her request for a serviceman. All her food, including her Easter ham, had spoiled.

In desperation, she went to the offending store and, to her surprise, found a knowledgeable, understanding manager, who offered to refund the entire original purchase price of her lemon. She picked out another less expensive model, which left her with enough money for some fun house paint and a new kitchen countertop. But it doesn't end here.

The next day, as she was driving to the grocery, smoke began to billow from her car in a frightening black cloud. She pulled over and called AAA (a miracle organization itself), who came and towed her to a service garage. The price to fix her car was another $300. But it doesn't end here.

The next day, the appliance store called to tell her they had misquoted the price of her new refrigerator by $300—in her favor! God had given her the money for a new refrigerator and a car that did not smoke, plus some left over.

Ellie loves Diet Cokes. I told her she could now get several Diet Cokes, drive around in her repaired car, and store what she doesn't drink in her new working refrigerator, then thumb through magazines picking out paint colors and granite. We also agreed that a huge "Thank you, God!" was in order. This story ends here.

Cataracts Of The Soul

Your eye is like a lamp that provides light for your body. When your eye is healthy, your whole body is filled with light. But when your eye is unhealthy, your whole body is filled with darkness. And if the light you think you have is actually darkness, how deep that darkness is!

Matthew 6:22-23 NLT

Cataracts creep up. They yellow your vision. You don't even know it. Only after the gift of new lenses do you see stark white, new light. It is the same with your soul. We as Christians seek the light. Yet with the changing of diapers, the hectic pace of soccer practice, the late nights of laundry, our eyes slowly and imperceptibly turn from God.

We fight with our spouse. The lines of love become blurred. Disappointments smear our vision with a displeasing shade of gray. We know things are not right, but we don't know what's wrong. Nothing is awful, nothing is wonderful.

It's during these times of nothingness that we must do something to restore the light of our soul, to seek His face. These are the times God gives us to drop to our knees, raise our clouded eyes to meet His, and ask Him for forgiveness, peace, clarity, and a new sight on Him. When we do, we will be reminded of the Johnny Nash song, "I Can See Clearly Now." There's gonna be a bright, bright sunshiny day!

Caught In The Act

Young people, it's wonderful to be young! Enjoy every minute of it. Do everything you want to do; take it all in. But remember that you must give an account to God for everything you do.

Ecclesiastes 11:9 NLT

Teen-aged boys these days! What can you do with them? One thing you might do on a snowy day is look out your window and see them shoveling your driveway—without being asked, without expecting to be paid.

You might pay them anyway, or at least offer them a cup of hot chocolate for them to wrap their red-cold hands around. Who knows, they might even be grateful and say, "Thank you." Then they will trudge back out, pull their collars up, throw a couple snowballs, then pick up their shovels and scrape away, while giggling and shouting good-natured insults at each other.

Yes, today they were caught in the act—the act of unselfishness and responsibility. So what you can do with them is brag on them, love on them, and pray for them. Those teen-aged boys today!

Convicted

Then I heard the voice of the Lord, saying, "Whom shall I send? And who will go for us?" And I said, "Here am I. Send me!"

Isaiah 6:8 NIV

In our church, there is a group of loving ladies, especially Nancy, called to a young women's jail ministry. I admit I have had little sympathy. "They got themselves into this pickle with their bad choices," I clucked to myself. My heart was hardened to their predicament.

Then, as I listened to jail ministry reports, I began to feel a gradual softening. Had I never made a mistake, especially in my youth? What if God had tossed me aside in my sins and indiscretions, and told me I was not worth saving? These young ladies have been convicted of crimes, yes. But God was daily and more persistently convicting me in my heart.

Yesterday, I received an e-mail asking for someone to come to next week's jail session and give the devotional. I felt a tugging. Today, my devotional was called, "Finding Strength In Life's Fire Swamps". The teaching was addressed to those who have found themselves in life's sucking swamps and who need God's help to slog out—completely appropriate for the jail ladies.

Some days I can't get anything to print from my aging computer. "Okay, God," I uttered, "If you want me to do this, please let the devotional print out." I never believed it would, but that printer spat that devotional out right in my face!

"Why me, Lord?" I questioned, as Isaiah did. I don't know. I do know that Isaiah next said, "Here I am. Send me." So, like Isaiah, I am getting ready to go. And I know I will be blessed in the conviction.

Culling

Therefore they will be like the morning cloud. And like dew which soon disappears. Like chaff which is blown away from the threshing floor. And like smoke from a chimney.

Hosea 13:3 NASB

On 9/16/16, a guest editor for our local *State Journal* wrote a letter titled "The Art of Culling". According to Webster's Dictionary, he explained, cull is "something rejected as being inferior or worthless." So, to cull is to rid ourselves of the inferior or worthless.

While I believe that no one is entirely worthless, there comes a time when we should consider culling those people or things in our lives that are keeping us from being where we should be in our walk with God.

I must admit I have become addicted to online yard sales. I spend too much time scrolling through items of no use to me, when I could be reading my Bible or baking for my family. I spend money on trinkets that, even though they are good bargains, gobble money that I could be giving to my church or the soup kitchen. I have asked God's help and forgiveness.

Sometimes we might be stuck in a toxic relationship. I had a long-time friend who was always ready to help when I needed him. He was also sardonic, looked for the worst in people, and one day betrayed a confidence of mine. With much sadness, I elected to cull our friendship. I miss him, and I bear him no ill will; yet for my peace I had to let him go.

What do you have that needs culling? Don't be hasty, pray about your situation, but if it warrants culling, empty it from your life. Peace will reign.

Customer Service Representative

Do not be anxious about anything, but in every situation, by prayer and petition, with thanksgiving, present your requests to God.

Philippians 4:6 NIV

Growing bored in retirement, on a whim, I applied to be a make-up consultant at a local department store. The job was not the most stressful or high-powered, but I still wanted to do well. It was freeing to not need a job, but to work for fun and a little extra money.

My interview was today. After being self-employed for 20 years, I was a bit apprehensive about being interviewed. I opened my copy of *The Upper Room.* Today's devotional was about—customer service representatives!

The importance of good customer service was stressed; the writer also stated it is essential that we pray for the little things, as well as the big. So I did. The interview went well. I was going to be hired. However, a back condition prevented me from being on my feet, as the job required. Still, I felt good. Even the interview was fun. I got to meet some of the other representatives—and I got to take home a few samples. It was a good day.

Dealing With Difficulty

The wise have wealth and luxury, but fools spend whatever they get.

PROVERBS 21:20 NIV

Dr. Phil, in his sermon, "How To Deal With Difficulty", reminded us that any trouble that happens is caused by one of four things: 1. Ourselves, 2. Other People, 3. Satan, or 4. God.

1. I once had a thriving business, but never in the summer of my life did I think to save any money I earned. Then I foolishly sold that business.
2. Following that came the discovery that my secretary had embezzled $65,000.
3. After that came a series of devastating human betrayals, the most difficult of all to bear. Now, in the fall/winter of my life, God has shown me that I must do without things I used to buy with impunity. But I sometimes grow tired of his correction. Last week, I splurged three times. Within days of my indiscretions, I received three unexpected bills for almost exactly the amount of my purchases. Now that is a swift consequence.
4. God has spoken clearly; it is up to me to obey. And so I confess it, confront it, deal with the aftermath, and claim the promise of God's care. Thankful for the merciful care and love of my Father God, I vow to serve Him with respect and honor, and I promise to be as wise as the ant.

Deliver Them From Evil

Then they cried out to the Lord in their trouble, and He delivered them from their distress.

Psalm 107:6 NIV

At 10:28 a.m. on Thursday, October 1, 2015, a 911 call rang out from a small Oregon Community college. A 26-year-old student had unleashed a barrage of bullets on a classroom full of students and two professors. He ordered them to the floor, then ordered them to stand one-by-one. He asked them individually, "Are you a Christian?" If they answered yes, he said, "Good. I will send you to God." And he shot them in the head.

When we think of religious persecution, we think of Syria, the Middle East, ISIS beheadings, but this day the ultimate religious persecution came to Roseburg Community College. In the face of abject terror, the students, some as young as 16, stood and proclaimed allegiance to God. So, the homegrown terrorist of the day got what he wanted. He killed them to this life, but with his evil act delivered them directly into the loving arms of the God they claimed.

What would you have done? Jesus died for you; would you die for Him? We would all like to think we would have answered, "I AM A CHRISTIAN!" This story is an invitation to us to pray and ask God for the strength to stare evil in the eye and face it down. They said yes. They are now where there is no pain, fear, or evil. So, for that, praise God for sending them home, even if their time here was just a second in eternity. We only hope we would be so brave.

For I Am With You

Don't be afraid, for I am with you. Don't be discouraged, for I am your God. I will strengthen you and help you. I will hold you up with my victorious right hand.

Isaiah 41:10 NLT

In the aftermath of 9/11/2001, French soldiers placed a large American flag at the foot of the Eiffel tower and stood at attention on either side. Last night, Friday, November 15, 2015, terror struck again, this time in Paris. A bloody total of 129 dead and 300+ wounded, for no reason other than believing in God.

Our enemies can do any manner of evil against us. They can shoot us, blow us up, behead us, even crucify us. But the suffering that Christians endure is swift, compared to the eternity that awaits us if we stand up for ourselves and our God. So today let us stand in holy formation for our fallen allies. May our governments finally say, "Enough is enough!" And while we are stunned this morning, we can be thankful for the most wonderful gift we have been given—and that is OUR GOD. Let us loudly proclaim Him. Praise God!

The Page

Do not seek revenge or bear a grudge against one of your people, but love your neighbor as yourself. I am the Lord.

Leviticus 19:18 NIV

Even on 9/11/2001, God left signs of hope in the midst of so much death and destruction. One symbol is the "iron cross" made from 2 pieces of the World Trade Center fused together into the shape of a cross. The *New York Times* reported a lesser known, but stunning, religious artifact. During excavation of the rubble, a chunk of the World Trade Center was found with a Bible page fused onto it. What was more astounding is the preserved verse: Ye have heard that it hath been said, An eye for an eye, and a tooth for a tooth: But I say unto you, That ye resist not evil: but whosoever shall smite thee on thy right cheek, turn to him the other also (Matthew 5:38-39 KJV).

Our country was crying for revenge on that day, but that verse was reminding us that perhaps revenge isn't always the best path—a thought hardly like those of us humans. Said a photographer on ground zero, "This shredded, burned and rubble-covered Bible came to me from the loving hands of a fireman who knew that I was the record keeper. My astonishment at seeing that particular page made me realize that the Bible's message survives throughout time. And in every era we interpret its teachings freshly, as the occasion demands." God spoke that day, on a tablet, no less.

I myself saw that Bible page at the Shanksville 9/11 Memorial in 2011, ten years after the heinous act. It still elicited fresh feelings of rage, but also comfort. As they died, the terrorists cried, "Allah Akbar!" On some level, they won. But God reminded us that He is the ultimate leader for eternity and we are the ultimate winners. Praise you, God!

Dreaded CEUs

Do not be slothful in zeal, be fervent in spirit, serve the Lord.

Romans 12:11 ESV

I had turned in my three continuing education units, a requirement for disability advocates. Only trouble was I turned in the wrong sessions. A nice woman named Kimberly called to say I had just 24 hours to read, synopsize, and electronically submit three new ones.

I was lacking in zeal. What I was not lacking in was agitation, anger, frustration and the beginnings of a stress headache. I did not want to watch boring webinars. I did not want to spend my evening reading 10 pages of the ever-so-fascinating Code of Federal Regulations.

I said a couple bad words as my mouth contorted into a pouty prune. I had done what I was supposed to do; it was not my fault that the CEU folks had given me the wrong courses. Besides, I had just had cataract surgery yesterday.

"Stupid CEUs," I childishly muttered to myself. I settled onto the couch with a glass of White Castle sweet tea beside me and began the laborious reading task. As I read, I realized how well I could see. The boring pages stood out vividly in crisp black and white. Before yesterday they would have been a blur, and I would not have been able to read them. What a miracle modern medical techniques are! I sent up a sincere and apologetic thank you to my God, who had restored my vision.

God's wonderful work was carried out by the hands of a mortal physician. If God could craft such miraculous work, then surely I could finish my mundane courses. I would do the work for God, my healer and rescuer. And I did. And I beat the deadline.

Feeding The Masses

...Taking the five loaves and the two fish and looking up to heaven, he gave thanks and broke the loaves...They all ate and were satisfied...

MATTHEW 14:19-20 NIV

It was our Sunday school class's turn to cook Wednesday night dinner. Our beloved sister, cook, and organizer, Joan White, was in charge. Because everyone loved Joan's BBQ, we had been told to make enough to feed 70 people. So we expected 70 people.

However, in the middle of preparations, Joan was told that 29 more members and child care workers wanted to eat. But wait—that was 99 hungry folks! It was too late to run out and buy more food. The kitchen help volunteered to give up our dinner. There was always bologna at home.

"We must make do," Joan confidently and calmly announced to her crew. And make do we did! "Cut the desserts in half," we were told. She instructed us to spoon out every morsel of meat. "Put a little less BBQ on each bun, a few less potato chips on each plate. Fill 'em up with extra beans!" commanded Joan.

Many souls were fed that night. All were served with love and a lot of scrimping. Nobody noticed the scarcity of BBQ, the plethora of beans, or the shrunken pieces of cake. Unbeknownst to us, God had pre-determined the number of guests and given us Joan to work her stretching magic. All 99 of us stood and gave thanks (especially us workers.) Then everyone dug in—and the masses were fed.

Green Bananas

> *But let all you who take refuge in You rejoice; let them sing joyful praises forever. Spread your protection over them, that all who love your name may be filled with joy. For You bless the godly, O Lord; you surround them with your shield of love.*
>
> Psalm 6:11-12 NLT

The banana was a bit green. I wanted it anyway. When I tried to peel it, the yellow skin tore off in a thin layer. Underneath was a strong white fibrous second skin, a part of the banana I had never seen. As I pulled it, it stubbornly clung to the banana.

We are like that banana. While still green, God will gently peel back the outer layers of our understanding, while he swaddles us in a stronger protective skin. At times when we feel frightened, untrusting, vulnerable, betrayed, or weak, we cannot see that extra protective blanket God has wrapped around us.

Still, rest easy in it, praying and praising God. When we are ripe in his word, he will gently remove the barrier, and reveal to us the fruit of life, and the strength to live it. So next time you feel afraid, peel a green banana and thank God for his unseen protection.

Milquetoast Christians

Anyone who lives on milk, being still an infant, is not acquainted with the teaching about righteousness. But solid food is for the mature, who because of practice have their senses trained to discern good and evil.

Hebrews 5:13-14 NIV

Do you remember when you brought home your first baby, that adorable innocent being? Perfect—until 2 a.m. Then you discovered the selfish shrieks of hunger, startling you from your rare sleep. In his way, your baby let you know: "I am in this world now, and it's all about me! And now!"

Your precious bundle did not give a hoot about your needs. He wanted what he wanted. So, by golly, you gave it to him. His contorted angry face turned angelic again, as you offered him the nipple. His little arms and legs curled into themselves. He guzzled. He was happy in his world, at all cost to you. You gave him milk because you loved him, because he would choke if you tried even semi-solid food.

Gradually, you introduced soft cereal to his palate. Not being accustomed to the consistency, he balked, looked at you as if you were a traitor, then made you laugh as his tongue and lips began to work in unison, leaving more cereal on the tray than in his mouth. Another six months and he graduated to finger foods and finally table food. No more packing milk, cereal, and baby food to the restaurant. Even when he was a toddler, you had to offer him small portions, so he didn't put too much in his mouth and choke.

And so it is with us as Christians. Even when we believe we have progressed to adulthood, we still have quarreling, selfishness, and doubts. We are still too much in the world.

Perhaps we will never reach Christian adulthood, but we strive. Some days we are "big people" Christians, chomping on filet mignon; other days we are reminded that we are God's little children, still chewing on milquetoast. We are children He loves, but who must strive to grow to the solid food of mature understanding. Still we practice.

Functional Obsolescence

So don't be misled, my dear brothers and sisters. Whatever is good and perfect is a gift coming down to us from God our Father, who created all the lights in the heavens. He never changes as a shifting shadow does.

JAMES 1:16-17 NLT

It was the first phrase I learned in real estate school in 2008, the year of the market crash. Nice timing, huh? I loved saying it, and I still do. It makes me feel smart. You try it, see? Functional Obsolescence! Fun to say, but not to live with. It means you might have the best house on the block, but if the surrounding houses/neighbors are less that desirable, you don't have much of a bargain.

I learned that when I bought an adorable gray Cape Cod cottage with dormers and a red door. The curb appeal was welcoming; the inside looked like *Southern Living*. I was so deliriously happy to have found such a darling home, that I agreed to an easement to a rental property to the side of mine. *Never* accept an easement!

Soon, the neighbors from you-know-where moved into the rental. They cursed, they abused their children, they let their pit bull roam through my yard, they walked through my yard, they drove through my yard. Eventually, they drove me out.

Look at the people in your life. Are there some who look and act enticing; who promise, but never deliver; who lie and cheat, who refuse to accept God? Are you in a work situation that is profitable, but not ethical? Is there an attitude or sin inside you that is spoiling your happiness? Walk away.

God might have allowed functional obsolescence into your life, because He gave you free will, but He will also give you discernment and the strength to disentangle yourself. We can still enjoy saying functional obsolescence. But say good-bye to any real functional obsolescence that is hindering your life, and you will be at peace.

Garbage Days

"For I know the plans I have for you", declares the Lord, "plans to prosper you and not to harm you, plans to give you a hope and a future."

JEREMIAH 29:11 NIV

Corrie Ten Boom said, "Faith sees the invisible, believes the unbelievable, and receives the impossible."

It was trash day. I stepped out onto the back porch, hidden by bushes. A large black dog was feasting on my next-door-neighbor's garbage bag. "Get out of there!" I yelled, while clapping my hands. The dog heard me, but after looking around and not seeing me, he went back to his pilfering.

This happened two more times, me yelling and clapping a little louder, and coming closer to the dog each time. Both times, he heard me, stopped again and looked around, and went back to the garbage. The next time, I stepped out of the bushes, where he could see me. Now when I told him to "get!", he reluctantly backed away from the bag, and slowly headed down the street, wanting desperately to get back to his nasty feast. Several times, he turned around to see if I was gone, but I continued to stand on the porch.

How many times have you heard God's call, faint at first, then louder and more persistent; yet you still want to go back to the "garbage" things in your life? God will keep calling and persisting, but He will not physically step out of the bushes into plain sight. This is where you must have faith.

God is here. He is with you. If you can hear His whispers, you must believe He is real. He is waiting patiently for you to get your nose out of the trash. He will be there with a feast far greater than any you could imagine. Now move away from the garbage and into the presence of your Abba. Your new life awaits!

Gimme Some Kinda Sign

By Debbie Smith

> *Blessed is the one who finds wisdom, and the one who gets understanding*
>
> Proverbs 3:13 ESV

How many times do you think God hears from us, "Give me a sign, please!" I'm guilty. I needed a sign! Our house was in need of repairs and I had to make a decision as to what contractor would do the best job. I had watched a home-remodeling company rebuild a house not far from me, from the ground up. Naturally, that was to be the starting place to begin my search.

Hopefully, the owners would be friendly and enlighten me about that company's expertise. Wary of strangers myself, I approached the house tentatively. There was no sign of life, as I peered through the glass door front. I tapped gently.

Out of nowhere, a cacophonous herd of dogs catapulted through the dining room, skittered across the living room floor and plastered themselves against the door. An eighth-inch of glass separated their snarling snouts from my face, agog with terror. I carefully backtracked down the porch steps and trotted at a fast clip across the yard and back to the safety of my car, yipping and yapping ringing in my ears. As I revved my car and slid quickly out of the driveway, I professed, "Uh, Lord, I will take that as a 'NO'!"

Good News

How difficult it is for me to fathom your thoughts about me, O God! How vast is their sum total!

Psalm 139:1 NIV

Claudette had been fretting and was a little down in the dumps. It was a gloomy day, so she did what a lot of us women do to cheer ourselves up—she settled in to watch an old Turner Classic movie. The name of the movie was *Good News*, a dizzy romance about a college football star, a coed and the young librarian, starring June Allyson and Peter Lawford.

Claudette admitted it was hokey, but, then, that's the charm of those old black-and-white movies. She had escaped into a comedy, which had lifted her spirits. When the credits rolled, she discovered that the movie had been released in the year she was born. She could not explain why, but this comforted her. It was as if God had picked that particular movie at that very time to let her know He was thinking about her—her own piece of Good News.

His Eye Is On The Squirrel Too

That is why I tell you not to worry about everyday life—whether you have enough food and drink, or enough clothes to wear. Isn't life more than food, and your body more than clothing? Look at the birds. They don't plant or harvest or store food in barns, for your heavenly Father feeds them. And aren't you far more valuable to him than they are? Can all your worries add a single moment to your life?

MATTHEW 6:25-27 NLT

Looking out my bedroom window, I saw the fuzzy brown squirrel perched on the very edge of the slate roof next door. Suddenly, he took a giant leap onto a tree eight feet away, and made a flawless landing! How did he know exactly how far to leap and where to grab on to the shaky branch? He had launched without fear. Without prayer, without knowing of God, his maker, he had leapt with perfect precision.

You or I could never have accomplished what the little squirrel did that day. We were made with feet to walk and hands to do work. Yet so many times we fail to walk out in faith, or to reach out and seize the day.

God made each creature of the earth in its own way and for its own purpose. God gave the squirrel keen eyes, claws, a warm coat, and perfect balance to survive its outside existence. He gave us the ability to think, to pray, to act wisely and in accordance with His commandments.

God created us all; He will surely keep a protective eye on us all. So say a little prayer, then take a leap of faith today. God will land you where He wants you.

Holy, Holy, Holy!

Holy, holy, holy is the Lord almighty; the whole earth is full of his glory!

Isaiah 6:3 NIV

"Please turn to page 64 in your hymnals, to Holy, Holy, Holy." How many times have we offered that beautiful song of love up to God, accompanied by the angelic voices of the choir and the instrumentalists playing their souls out for the Lord?

Being a Bible dilettante, I never knew those words were first written by the prophet, Isaiah, when the Lord showed him a vision of angels with six wings, singing these words to each other. Cherubim and seraphim… So powerful were their voices of worship that the doors shook and the temple was filled with smoke. God had given orders to Isaiah to lead the people of Judah. Isaiah was afraid, yet without hesitation, he answered the calling, saying, "Here I am, send me!"

Have you ever been afraid, lacking faith in your abilities? Is there somewhere God is leading you, and you are ignoring the call? Can you, like brave Isaiah, say to God, "Here I am, send me!"

Be assured the Lord will guide you, and you will be surrounded by protective cherubim and seraphim. Maybe it won't be easy, but your Lord God almighty will show you the way. What greater instructor can you have than your holy God and his angels?

Sing it out loud, "Holy, holy, holy, Lord God almighty!" Worship him completely, then totally obey, and let Him send you!

I'd Lie And Go Hide In The Closet

...for all have sinned and fall short of the glory of God, and are justified freely by his grace through the redemption that came by Christ Jesus.

ROMANS 3:23-24 NIV

While trying to teach my sons and their little friends a moral lesson, I asked them if they knew what they would do if they knew they had sinned. One said he would be sorry, one told me he would ask forgiveness, another said he would confess to his parents. Then, I suspect the most honest answer came from a little brown-eyed boy, who blurted out, "I'd lie, and go hide in the closet!"

In our Bible study, we are reading Genesis, interspersed with the other books. This week's lesson is sin. *Sin.* Ouch! Everything was great, until that word was put into action by the very first man and woman God made. They had it all, but they could not obey the only rule God gave them. Thus, they set into motion a catastrophe of punishment and shame. And when they sinned, they ran and hid.

The word "hide" is predominant in this lesson. Genesis 3:8, "and they hid from the Lord God." Psalm 19:12, "Forgive my hidden faults." Admit it, we perform our forbidden behavior in hiding, not in the light of day, where all can see.

After we sin and remorse sets in, we want to run and hide—not literally in a closet, but our heart crouches and hides from God. Yet, as Adam and Eve couldn't escape, neither can we. We might fool every man and woman on earth, but we can't fool God—and why would we want to deprive ourselves of God's glorious face?

God gives us free will and its consequences. He also gives us mercy and compassion. Don't lie and hide and run for the closet. Next time we sin, let's run straight to our God, fall at His feet, say we're sorry, and sin no more. Come on out. Accept God's amazing grace.

In The Midst

Be joyful in hope, patient in affliction, faithful in prayer.

Romans 12:12 NIV

Margaret's father-in-law, Dan, was 92 and in the last stages of metastatic bone cancer. Prayers for healing had gone unanswered. A few weeks earlier, he had been still walking with a walker, but his condition was rapidly deteriorating, so that by the next week, he was bedridden.

His pain had become debilitating. Hospice was called in. Those angels of mercy came and administered compassionate doses of morphine. Margaret, her daughter-in-law, Elsie, and her son, Tim, were taking turns caregiving—an exhausting, but holy duty.

Feeling weary, but trying to keep their smiles on, they gathered around Dan. The silence around a death bed can be deafening. To make conversation, Tim asked, "Papaw, how are you feeling?"

Dan's face brightened and his glazed eyes cleared. "With all of you here, how could I not feel better?!" Papaw Dan, in the midst of his suffering, was a happy man because he was surrounded by those he loved the most—and so were Margaret, Elsie, and Tim. Blessed they all were.

Into The Pouch

You will again have compassion on us; you will tread our sins underfoot and hurl all our iniquities into the depths of the sea.

MICAH 7:19 NIV

Have you ever found a shell and thrown it into the ocean? If you did, do you imagine that you will ever see or feel that shell again? That would be impossible. The ocean swallows it into its vast mouth.

So it is with our sin. We can carry the shells of guilt and shame around with us every day, growing heavier with the burden. Or we can pack those sins up and toss them away forever.

Think of your worst sin(s). Write it down. Ask God to forgive it. Then put your "sin" into a bag and drop it into a sink of hot water (or the ocean, if you are there.) Watch it fade as it dissolves into illegible shreds. Now, just like that, God has made you sins illegible in the Book of Life, and it is as if they never happened. You are forgiven!

It's Hard To Be Mad When You're Wearing Squeaky Shoes

As a father has compassion on his children, so the Lord has compassion on those who fear him...

Psalm 103:13 NIV

Today I saw a Facebook video showing a little Asian girl exhibiting the universal three-year-old pout, arms clasped tightly across her chest, head down, lower lip out. When her dad, the object of her derision, spoke to her, she would turn her back on him. Trouble was, daddy had bought her shoes that made a happy, squeaky sound when she moved.

She tried to stay mad. She really did. But soon the happy squeaking sounds caused her to break into a grin, then a full-fledged laugh. She began a gleeful dance, hands in the air, twirling, squeaking, and forgiving with each step.

It would be inappropriate for us, as adults, to do the three-year-old pout. But do we ever give our spouse the silent treatment or a cold shoulder? In our frustration with our teenagers, do we often purse our lips in disapproval? What about when your own three-year-old is pouting, or has just powdered your kitchen floor with flour? Does that child see our disapproval as we raise our hands in despair?

Did your friend say something that hurt your feelings, and you haven't called her for days? Warm that cold shoulder, lower your arms to hug the errant child. Erase the prune lips and instead offer your teenager a kiss on the cheek (if he will allow it). Pick up the phone.

But how to forgive, you ask? Quite simple. Just imagine you are wearing squeaky shoes. Now start dancing.

Lead Us In Prayer

When you pray, do not keep babbling on like pagans, for they think they will be heard because of their many words. Do not be like them, for your Father knows what you need before you ask Him! This, then, is how you should pray: (The Lord's Prayer).

MATTHEW 6:7-13 NIV

"(Your name here), would you lead us in prayer?"

Do these words strike heart-racing fear in you? Why? Prayer is just talking to God. We all do that, hopefully, throughout the day. He is our father, friend, counselor—all easy persons to talk to rolled into One.

Yet for some of us, praying in public feels as if we are addressing the audience only. Our throats close, our mouths dry. We need a drink of water and a deep breath. I once knew a man so frightened at having been called upon to say a public prayer, that he never went back to church. Hopefully, our fear is not as severe as his.

Why don't we forget our earthly audience and pretend we are at home and just say to God what is on our hearts? Our sermon today, "Rivers of Prayer", helped us understand our own personal style of prayer. Whether we are going to worship, confess, thank, supplicate, intercede, or ask forgiveness—just say it. We are challenged to shake up our status quo and to risk stretching out of our prayer comfort zone.

I pray about praying. I would so love to open my mouth and pour out an eloquent prayer, but that is not my style; I prefer simple words. But I can take a deep breath, a deep gulp, close my eyes, open my mouth, and let rivers of my heart flow out. You can too. We can all do that.

Dear Father God...

Little Pigs

When the demons came out of the man, they went into the pigs, and the herd rushed down the steep bank into the lake and drowned.

Luke 8:33 NLT

We all strive for a pure heart, to be perfect and blameless, like Jesus. We all fail. I admit it. In spite of my intentions, I sometimes spew forth bad words. Never God's name in vain, but still impure words said in frustration. I immediately regret them and ask God's forgiveness. Still, those little "demon words" seem to possess my tongue.

Today I begged God to help me quit. He led me to Luke 8:33. He told me to imagine each bad word flying out of my mouth and into a little pink pig, tumbling over a cliff and disappearing into a deep lake.

With God's help, there will be fewer and fewer little leaping pigs until the day I am strong enough to cast those creatures off my lips and out of my life into a bottomless pit, never to be heard again. Thank you, Lord, for your patience and guidance.

Little Black Pony

Give honor to marriage, and remain faithful to one another in marriage.

HEBREWS 13:4 NLT

Marcia's husband, Chris, had a favorite book as a boy. He would go to the school library and check it out for as long as possible, take it back, then immediately check it out again— again and again. Even as an adult, he spoke so fondly of it that Marcia decided to find him a copy of *The Little Black Pony.*

She began an online search, but found prices to be over $100 at virtually every site. She couldn't justify paying so exorbitantly, so she ended her search. A few years later, she was rummaging through some of her old childhood treasures. There were her favorite Bobbsey Twins and Nancy Drew series. But what fell out of the stack of her girly books astounded her. The book! *The Little Black Pony*!

She had had it all those years, and forgotten about it. With a heart full of love, she wrapped the book and gave it to Chris, her answer to a prayer she didn't even realize she had prayed. Maybe you are looking for something in your life—an answer from God, and it's there in the stack of your worries and wishes. Don't be surprised when your "Little Black Pony" falls out onto God's pages, from God's stack of blessings on you.

Make Thy Way Plain

Fear of the Lord is the foundation of true wisdom. All who obey His commandments will grow in wisdom. Praise Him forever!

Psalm 111:10 NLT

I was reading a daily devotional on my phone one evening, and I was tired. The letters seemed to merge into jumbles, and I couldn't concentrate. Through my fatigue, though, I knew there was a message for me, but my eyes were barely open.

Suddenly, an unusual pop-up appeared on my screen. It looked like a test page for my printer. It instructed me to press PRINT for one copy. I could not even tell what I was being instructed to copy, but I pushed PRINT anyway, then fell asleep.

The next morning, in my printer, was a copy of the devotional from the night before! I cut out the first sentence and taped it to my mirror, and read it daily for weeks. "MAKE THY WAY PLAIN BEFORE MY FACE." Psalm 5:8.

Nothing much changed. What I had not done, was what the message of Proverbs 16:3 commanded: "COMMIT TO THE LORD WHATEVER YOU DO, and He will establish your plans." I had only asked for the answers; I had failed to commit my decisions and doubts to Him first.

It is about giving up control, not barreling through our days, making decisions by ourselves, and not just making out our wish list, telling God what to do. I guess God knew I was nodding off, but He knew more that I needed this lesson, so He saved it for me. For that, I praise Him!

Money Worries

And if God cares so wonderfully for wildflowers that are here today and thrown into the fire tomorrow, he will certainly care for you. Why do you have so little faith? So don't worry about these things, saying, "What will we eat? What will we drink? What will we wear?" These things dominate the thoughts of unbelievers, but your heavenly Father already know all your needs.

MATTHEW 6:30-32 NLT

Ten years ago, I sometimes made as much money in one month as I now receive in one year from my Social Security pension. I owned a lucrative business. My husband and I made yearly trips to Jamaica. He bought me rubies and diamonds. I shopped in boutiques. I drove around in his Mercedes. It was my Cinderella decade.

But circumstances change. Husbands die, people betray you, health declines, houses fall down, kids need help. You make your own foolish decisions. Now I sometimes find myself going without, so I can buy food for my children. The worrying has given me stomach problems, which means I need another expensive medication.

I am still in my financial season of worry. Yet I still have what I need. No spending extravaganzas, but a little left over for small indulgences, like eating out occasionally.

Through my hardships, God has shown me that with discipline I can get by with less. After yesterday's morning prayer, God told me to go through my checkbook. I did that and was surprised at how much I still fritter away.

So I will cut back some more. I still worry, but I'm still here. I have always been taken care of, sometimes not as I would like, but always as I need. My God has given me the beauty of this day, and my daily bread.

My End Table

For we are God's masterpiece.

Ephesians 2:10 NLT

God is giving me words today. He is giving me rain and thunder as the perfect atmosphere for thinking and writing. I gather my treasures—Bible, devotionals, pen, papers, coffee, and set them on the table beside me.

I bought this old Shaker-style table when it was newly refinished in pine with oak inlays. There are drawers on each end, with white ceramic knobs, the perfect places to store my pencils and musings. The base is pyramid-shaped.

The shop owner told me that when he took the table apart to refinish it, he found a note from the maker, dated 1923. Such beautiful workmanship! I was so proud of my table. I forbade anyone to put a glass or cup on it; no food was allowed on it.

Then one day, baby Sophia set her Icee on it. Pink water melted into and stained my beautiful table. And so it began, the decline of my perfect table.

Today there are only patches of unspoiled finish on the top. The rest has long ago been eroded. Chunks of inlay have fallen away. But now we're old friends, my table and I. We share our early mornings and rainy days and our seasons.

I grace my faded table with my special belongings. It holds my cup agreeably for me. There is no fear of ruining the table. It is worn and aging, as I am, but like two old shoes, we are familiar. My old table, like me, is still handy and hospitable, imperfect, but better with age. And we were both made by master craftsmen.

No Big Deal, But...

Trust in the Lord with all your heart and lean not on your own understanding. Seek His will in all you do, and He will show you which path to take.

PROVERBS 3:5-6 NLT

It had taken a few days more than I had anticipated to compose a brief to the judge in one of my Social Security disability cases, so I was delayed in submitting it. Time was of the essence. When I put it in my ailing fax machine, that dreaded screeching sound emitted, indicating a significant problem with the connection.

Three times it jammed; three times I removed the back of the fax machine and removed the errant paper. I am basically fax-illiterate, so I resorted to hitting that machine, the only other tactic I knew, and a ploy that sometimes actually worked. No luck. I did not know what else to do. Desperation was setting in.

Admitting my ignorance and helplessness, I cried to God, "God, please let this go through." I pushed send again. The machine rattled ominously, then settled down. Smoothly and quietly, it sent my fax! I had spent the entire morning trying to solve my problem on my own when all I had to do was ask God for help.

Old Faithful

The earth is the Lord's, and everything in it. The world and all its people belong to Him. For He laid the earth's foundation, on the seas and built it on the ocean depths.

PSALM 24:1 NLT

The famous geyser in Yellowstone National Park, Wyoming, was nicknamed Old Faithful in 1870 because it is one of the most predictable geographical features on Earth, erupting every 63 seconds. Over 1 million eruptions have been recorded.

God is more faithful than our earthly Old Faithful. He is faithful all the time, for every person on Earth. His faith in us is infinite, immeasurable. It is impossible for humans to be 100 percent faithful in all things 100 percent of the time. That's why our God has given us mercy and grace. We as mortals are to figuratively forgive at least 70 x 7; God forgives us 1 million x 1 million times, if we repent and ask.

God's geyser of forgiveness is bottomless and erupts with 100 percent predictability, covering us in His love, a love which is stretched as far as the east is from the west. It is so hard to imagine such an omnipresent love, but God's love is given to us, not every 63 seconds, but every second of every day, no matter which part of the Earth we inhabit. How powerful! We are all his children, and our Yahweh is faithful to us here and for eternity.

The One-Room Cabin

> *The Lord is my shepherd. I shall not want. He makes me lie down in green pastures, He leads me beside quiet waters, He restores my soul.*
>
> Psalm 23:1-3 NIV

The one-room cabin was advertised in the paper. On a whim, I responded. It had no electricity; it had no running water; it had to be moved 15 miles out in the country to my 56 acres. There was every good reason not to buy that cabin. Yet, again on a whim, I did just that.

A peace overwhelmed me when I stepped inside. The country has always been my haven, with its green fields, deep woods, velvet hills, and gentle creek. I had always dreamed of having a permanent place there to meditate.

I had my cabin set just at the edge of the woods. An electrician friend installed my electric. We purchased a used five-gallon water dispenser. Chad, who also has an affinity for the country, painted the inside a cheery yellow. We had fun furnishing it with garage sale finds. I even found curtains with squirrels and deer on them.

This cabin retreat has brought my family such pleasure. Yet, when I bought it, I could not have imagined that Chad would be downsized and become homeless for a while. Yes, this one-room cabin became a real home to him in his time of trouble. One night I asked him if he would like to stay in town with me. "Thanks, mom," he responded, "but I love it out there. I sleep so well with the dark and the sound of the creek flowing."

Thankfully, Chad's situation improved, and he has moved back to town, but that one-room cabin served a purpose that only God could have foreseen when I first stepped in the door.

The Rainbow
by Debbie Smith

Then I saw another mighty angel coming down from heaven, surrounded by a cloud, with a rainbow over his head.

Revelation 10:1 NLT

Wouldn't it be a perfect miracle, just like in a movie? I was in a plane flying high above the sunlit clouds the color of ecru satin. "Lord, if you would send me a rainbow over these clouds, wouldn't it be excellent? I kind of needed a rainbow, too. I was headed back home from visiting my nephew in California, and I was feeling just a little sad.

After riding in the clouds for some time, there was still no rainbow. I leaned my head against the cold window and closed my eyes. Was that too much to ask? Just one rainbow? From the Creator of the universe?

I sighed a wistful sigh and squinted against the sun rays filtering through the frosted window's edge. The reflection of the light on the glass broke the light into brilliant colors – making the perfect rainbow. My own personal rainbow. "Thank you, Lord!"

The Refund

Command those who are rich in this world not to be arrogant nor to put their hope in wealth, which is so uncertain, but to put their hope in God, who richly provides us with everything for our enjoyment.

1 Timothy 6:17 NIV

Every Friday is girl's day out for lunch. This particular Friday, I felt I shouldn't go because I had splurged on a fun orange lipstick. Accepting my self-imposed consequences, I was prepared to stay at home.

On Thursday, a letter, which looked ominously like a belated bill from my eye surgeon, arrived. I opened it with trepidation. Instead of a bill, it was a refund check from last year! The amount was $11.56—just enough for lunch with my friends.

I called my friends and told them I could join them after all. Johnny Carino's has a spicy lasagna and salad lunch special. I had that. The bill was $8.99, plus the tip, which I was only too happy to leave. God, You knew exactly how much I needed, and You provided it in a most timely, unexpected way.

The Apartment At Anguilla

by Margaret Maggard

I will always thank the Lord; I will never stop praising Him.
I will praise Him for what He has done.

Psalm 34:1-2 GNT

About five months ago, Danielle, our middle daughter, came to Frankfort to visit her dad and me, and she had some very exciting news. After having worked in the medical field as a drug representative for the past 10 years, Danielle had decided that she wanted to go to medical school and specialize in Addictive Medicine. In fact, she had already been accepted to the Saint James School of Medicine located on the island of Anguilla in the Caribbean.

Danielle arranged for her dad and me to travel with her to Anguilla to help her find a safe place to live for the next two years, and also find a car to rent. The day after Thanksgiving, Danielle and I travelled 11 hours and finally arrived on the beautiful island of Anguilla by ferry. Danielle's dad, Danny, would join us later the next evening.

When we awoke Saturday morning, we could see the lush green foliage and beautiful flowers outside the Villa. We heard a myriad of birds, and from the front porch, we could see the beautiful blue Caribbean Sea.

We just had time to drink our coffee and dress for the day, when Danielle and I heard a car's tires crunching the gravel outside our open windows. Danielle went out in the courtyard and introduced herself to Neville, whom her original property manager had arranged for her to meet. Neville had brought the keys to her rental car and her temporary license.

She invited Neville inside to meet me and to talk more to him about Anguilla. Neville asked Danielle what her objectives were for the next four days. She explained that the apartment she had originally rented four months ago had received major water damage this past summer and the property manager had called her last month to explain that because of mold and mildew and damaged furniture, the apartment would not be ready to rent this January. (She had promptly returned Danielle's deposit and also allowed us to stay in her lovely personal villa when we came for this trip.)

Danielle told Neville she was looking for a place to live, in a safe neighborhood, hopefully near the medical school. The monthly rent must be within her limited budget, and she needed to rent a small car for her two-year stay.

Neville looked right at my daughter and said, "Danielle, I can tell from our conversation this morning that you are a Christian. I have a large three-bedroom apartment above my house that you and your roommate may rent while you are in medical school. I do not allow drinking alcohol or partying in the apartment, but I know that you would not do that. I can just tell that you are a Christian, and your mother is smiling through her tears and nodding in agreement. I have all the assurance I need.

My house is in a very safe area of the island, and it is less than one mile from the Saint James School of Medicine. You both come see it today, and if you like it, I'll rent it to you for $900 a month, plus utilities." (This amount was much less than what Danielle had been quoted by several other property managers on the island.)

Four hours later, we met Neville at the School of Medicine and followed him the short distance to his two-story, turquoise concrete home. We instantly loved the place; it was furnished, and we could actually see the roof of the medical school from her apartment. Neville had been a policeman for 20 years and was now a security officer for one of the island's hotels. He said he would be like a father to Danielle and Marianna, her recently acquired roommate, who was a nurse from Tennessee.

I felt so good for Danielle, and I truly felt that this was all A GOD THING! Neville even found a small car from his rental car lot, for Danielle and Marianna to rent while they are in school.

GOD IS SO GOOD!

Danny arrived late Saturday, and he and Danielle made the trip on Sunday afternoon to meet Neville, see the huge apartment, pay the deposit and seal the deal.

GOD IS SO GOOD!

We are so grateful that Neville could see GOD's love in our daughter, Danielle. Please continue to pray for her as she begins this long journey to become a doctor.

POST SCRIPT: On September 6, 2017, Anguilla was decimated by hurricane Irma. Danielle's apartment was destroyed. The people of Anguilla are still struggling with loss of housing, utilities, and clean water. Please continue to pray for the residents. Another miracle for Danielle and her family is that she made it safely back to the states before the hurricane hit. She is safe, and plans to continue her studies here in the United States.

INDEED, GOD IS SO GOOD!

The Retirement Plan

...And love your neighbor as yourself.

MATTHEW 19:19 NIV

Ada Kay's daughter, Bonnie, had just retired from teaching. She and her husband, Dave, had had enough of the big city where they had spent their youth, with its snarling traffic and deteriorating school system. But their hearts were troubled at the prospect of leaving their long-time neighbor, Ed, who was now elderly and alone.

The solution was evident to Betty and Dave. They simply bought a big house in the peaceful mountains of Boone, North Carolina, with an extra room for their neighbor, and moved him into the house with them! They decided they would just all look after each other. What a Christian, generous thing to do!

Betty and Dave happily told the story of the move as if there was nothing unusual about it. Oh, and the local school board asked Bonnie if she wanted a job, so she's teaching in a little country school and loving it. And now Dave and Ed have someone to drink coffee and putter about with during the day—God's perfect retirement plan for Bonnie, Dave, *and* Ed.

Right Place, Right Time

So we keep on praying for you, asking our God to enable you to live a life worthy of the call. May He give you the power to accomplish all the good things your faith prompts you to do. Then the name of our Lord Jesus will be honored because of the way you live, and you will be honored along with Him. This is all made possible because of the grace of our God and Lord, Jesus Christ.

2 Thessalonians 1:11 NLT

Corky's son, Robbie, was in a wreck on rainy dark highway. He was injured, but still conscious and able to dial 911. In the meantime, a young man on his way to work at a factory stopped to assist Robbie. He asked Robbie if he wanted to pray. They did. The man stayed with Robbie until the medics arrived.

Later, the man and his family visited Robbie in the hospital. He told Robbie that one of his friends had been killed on that same stretch of highway the year before, and of how difficult it was to stop that day, but he had felt God prompting him. Maybe God was providing him with the catharsis he needed, and he chose to accept it. Today, that young man is pastor of Robbie's church, and they remain close friends.

Root Canals

So be truly glad. There is wonderful joy ahead, even though you must endure many trials for a little while. These trials will show that your faith is genuine. It is being tested as fire tests and purifies gold—though your faith is far more precious than mere gold. So when your faith remains strong through many trials, it will bring you much praise and glory and honor on the day when Jesus Christ is revealed to the whole world.

1 PETER 1:6-7 NLT

"I'd rather have a root canal." How many times have we said that? Today I had a root canal, and as I was tilted back with my mouth immobilized, unable to speak (a rarity), I began to consider the root canal.

First comes the slightly painful novocaine. Then the dentist begins to drill the dead enamel away, leaving just the outer shell of a tooth. He drills some more, an unpleasant sensation, as the annoying sound of the drill throws out pieces of tooth. Suction, spit, wipe.

With the tiny probe, he digs down into the root, removing the rotten pulp that has caused our pain, and replacing it with a greater momentary pain, as he hits a nerve—a searing pain that would make us bolt out of our chair, if we could. But then the worst is over. He withdraws the probe, replaces the decayed pulp with fresh, healthy material. Last, ever so skillfully, he crafts a new tooth to replace the drilled-away old one.

Isn't that like being refined? When our soul is hurting, it's a sign that we need to drill away at our outer selves until we reach the pulp of our despair, then root it out and replace it with a new life. This soul-gouging will be painful, but temporary and necessary. And when it's over, we will have a shiny, new heart in place of the pain.

The Scary Miracle

Have mercy on me, O God, have mercy on me, for in you my soul takes refuge. I will take refuge in the shadow of your wings until the disaster has passed.

Psalm 57:1 NIV

All was quiet; all was calm. Then it wasn't. It was two a.m. that April night in 2015. The ear-piercing fire alarm shrieked, frightening Aaron and Ashleigh from their peaceful slumber. Was it real? It was real! Their new house was on fire!

Flames and smoke spit venomously from the roof. Most terrifying was the complete engulfing of two-year-old Presleigh's room down the hall. The miracle: Because Presleigh was earlier afraid of a monster under her bed, Aaron and Ashleigh had allowed her to crawl into bed with them, where she was comforted and wrapped in the special blanket her great-grandmother, "Old Mamaw," had lovingly made for her—and where she remained, safely snuggled with mommy and daddy.

The family fled in the night, little Presleigh clutched crushingly tight in daddy's arms. Safely outside, they watched with dismay as the orange, angry flames lit up the black sky. Aaron and Ashleigh could also see those flames reflected in the wide eyes of Presleigh, as she stood now between them, still wrapped in the comfort of Old Mamaw's special blanket, frightened, but unharmed. Her precious life was saved by a common childhood fear. Thank you, God, for scary under-the-bed monsters.

Smile!

A glad heart makes a cheerful face.

Proverbs 15:13 ESV

As we entered the department store, we were greeted with a brilliant smile and a sincere "Hi!" The official store greeter, you might think. No, a delightful little dark-haired toddler with her nose pressed against the glass partition that separated incoming from outgoing customers. As she flashed her happy smile at each of us, we couldn't help but smile back and offer a big "hello" to her, as well.

How many times might we have freely given a smile to other shoppers? Why don't we? As adults, we lose our true expression and gain inhibitions. We fear being inappropriate; we fear rejection, we fear being politically incorrect. Sometimes we are just too busy, in a bad mood, or having a bad day.

But not our little greeter. She was without an agenda, other than joy. As her mother led her from the store, we heard her exclaim, "Mommy, I made people smile!" By giving of her true self, she had been blessed in return.

Ask God to remind you to smile at people you pass today. Then you can say, "Daddy, I made people smile!" And all will be blessed.

Smokey Joe

...And the scriptures give us hope and encouragement as we wait patiently for God's promises to be fulfilled.

ROMANS 15:4 NLT

Camille had Smokey Joe for 18 years. He was her beloved horse. For the past several years, she had kept him at her boyfriend's farm, where they rode together. Then the relationship ended. Camille was left with a broken heart and nowhere to keep Smokey Joe.

A few years back, she and her friend Julie had enjoyed riding, but Julie had moved to Tennessee. Julie had wanted to take Smokey Joe with her family, but they had no place for him to stay. In bleak January, with a broken heart, Camille was forced to board Smokey Joe in Bagdad, Kentucky, where she could not readily get to him. Boarding fees were $250 per month. So many losses in one year.

Then last Wednesday in Kroger, she saw a woman who looked like Julie. When she turned around, it was Julie! She and her family had just moved back to Frankfort. When Camille asked her if she was still interested in Smokey Joe, Julie was ecstatic. Julie has two children and needs a calm horse. That is old Smokey Joe! Now they are making arrangements to move him to Julie's farm.

Camille is sad, but she can still see her horse and ride with her friend, who will love Smokey Joe as she does. She is saving the boarding fee to buy a lot at the Guist Creek campground. The lot fee is $250 per month. Slowly, Camille is putting her past behind her and moving on to a different, but happier future. She can see God's work in her life—and she knows there is hope.

Speck In The Eye

Why do you look at the speck of sawdust in your brother's eye and pay no attention to the plank in your own eye? How can you say to your brother, "Let me take the speck out of your eye," when all the time, there is a plank in your own eye? You hypocrite, first take the plank out of your own eye, and then you will see clearly to remove the speck from your brother's eye.

MATTHEW 7: 3-5 NIV

The day was dreary and cold. My best friend had said something thoughtless, and I was upset with her. Besides that, something was in my eye. What was probably just an eyelash felt like a tree branch. At first, it was just annoying, but when all efforts to remove it failed, it became an obsession. "Gotta get rid of this! Gotta get rid of this!" I rubbed; I plucked. And still it stuck, hidden high in my upper eyelid. All day.

My eye turned red as the setting sun. Here it was nightfall, and still this thing in my eye taunted and irritated, until my vision blurred to white. Desperate, I remembered the old bottle of saline solution in the back of the medicine cabinet. I ran to the bathroom, grabbed the bottle, and poured a torrent into my eye.

I blinked hopefully a few times. Could it be?! It was gone! "Thank you, God!" I shouted to the empty room. So, when you have a day you feel you have nothing to be thankful for, just be thankful you don't have a speck in your eye.

Addendum:

The next morning, my Bible fell open to Matthew 7: 3-5!

I picked up the phone and called my friend.

The Still, Small Voice

He spoke in a "still small voice."

I Kings 19:12 Our Daily Bread Bible

Rosie's mother was very ill. She had been admitted to the hospital for heart surgery, the success of which was uncertain. After her mother was wheeled into the operating room, Rosie and her dad went straight to the hospital chapel to pray and calm their anxiety.

Other than a woman alone and sobbing, there was no one else inside the darkened room. The woman left. When Rosie and her dad were truly alone, they noticed that the sun lit the narrow cross of stained glass cut into the front of the chapel, as if a light switch had been flicked on, sending brilliant colors floating around the room.

Suddenly, Rosie heard a gentle voice say, "Your mother will be all right." Shaken and a bit stunned, she looked at her father, who was also a little unsettled.

"Did you hear that?" she asked. "A voice said she would be all right."

"Yes," her dad responded quietly.

Yes, they both had heard the comforting words, at the same time, unbeknownst to the other. Reassured, they smiled at each other, and knelt to thank God in advance.

Stinky Toes

...How beautiful are the feet of those who bring good news.

ROMANS 10:15 NIV

In our house, we have a book called, *How Many Stinky Toes?* Feet are certainly not considered our most beautiful asset. It seems God started at the top and worked his way down, setting our feet in the lowest place, close to the dirt.

Feet get no respect. Some are gigantic, LeBron James feet. Some are tiny, baby feet. Some have been too long in the socks. Some have calluses from walking around in life.

Feet support our entire body and take us everywhere we want to go. Sometimes they take us to the Grand Canyon, sometimes just to the kitchen to pour a cup of coffee. At times, they trudge to places of grief, of despair, to the valley of the shadow. Some days, they slide us through the muddy creek. Yes, sometimes feet are stinky.

But, oh, the beauty of the feet which run to announce the wedding, the birth of the baby, or the first daffodil! God knew what He was doing when He gave us lowly feet. Thank you, God, for good news and the feet that carry it. Thank you for beautiful, stinky toes!

The Talents

Again, it will be like a man going on a journey, who called his servants and entrusted his property to them. To one he gave five talents of money, to another two talents, and to another one talent, each according to his ability.

MATTHEW 25:14-15 NIV (TO READ THE WHOLE STORY, VISIT MATTHEW 25:1-30.)

We've all heard the story of the talents. The first man put his money to work and earned five more talents, so did the man with two talents; but the man with one talent ran and buried his for safekeeping. When the master returned, he was proud of the first two men for using their talents and expanding their wealth.

The one with only one talent was excited to tell that he had saved his. He expected the man to be proud of him. Instead, the man admonished him for not putting his money to work, calling him a wicked, lazy servant. The master took the one talent and gave it to the man with the five (now 10) talents.

Now, I have always had trouble with this story. On the one hand, we are told to save for a rainy day. So why was the man so angry upon his return? I believe the key word is not money, but Ability. God has given us all abilities. We have used some and surely wasted others.

I know a woman with an angelic voice, yet she refuses to bless her church by singing, saying her voice is not good enough. (1 Corinthians 14:12: Since you are eager to have spiritual gifts, try to excel in gifts that build up the church.) If we remain silent with the gift of song, or leave the canvas blank, or the homemade bread unmade, or the encouraging word unspoken, we are indeed saying to God, "This gift you have given me is not good enough." How saddened this must make Him. We have wasted our talent and insulted God greatly.

Would you accept a beautiful painting from a friend, then store it away in the cedar chest? It would hurt your friend and deny others the pleasure it was intended to give. It would belittle the fact that the gift was chosen especially for you. (1 Corinthians 7:7: But each man has his own gift from God; one has this gift; another has that.)

So, today get God's gift to you out of the cedar chest and enjoy it, display it, bake it, use it, say it, sing it. Whether your gift is "this or that," show God by your actions that you appreciate it.

The Tire Diaries (And Still Nothing Happened)

For it is by grace you have been saved...

Ephesians 2:8 NIV

June 16, 2016 Got new set of tires put on my car by (store name left blank to protect the guilty). Feeling good.

July 3, 2016 Passing motorist alerted me to low back left tire. My friend, Camille, and I stopped at an air station and figured out how to add air. Feeling irritated.

August 19, 2016 Went out to find totally flat right front tire. Called AAA, who put enough air in tire for me to make it back to ____________. After I sat in ____________ for three hours, they told me tire had not been properly sealed, but should be good to go now. No apology. Feeling very irritated.

September 15, 2016 Another low tire. Another call to AAA. More air added. Feeling agitated.

October 13, 2016 Three tires low. Chad added air to all three, plus the fourth tire for good measure. Feeling very vexed.

November, 2016 No flat tires! Feeling hopeful.

December 6, 2016 Walked out of house to find completely flat back left tire. Kind neighbor pumped it up once again, so I could get to ________________. Feeling borderline ballistic.

Back to________________, only this time took a man friend with me. Talked to alleged owner of ______________ this time, who admitted tires they put on in June were four sizes too small! Said it was a safety issue because tires were too small to hold weight of car. Apologized profusely to man friend. Also replaced old/new tires with new upgraded set. Apologized some more. Feeling vindicated.

ALL these days I was inconvenienced.
ALL these days I was angry.
ALL these days I was in danger.

Yet,
NONE of these days did I have a blowout while driving.
NONE of these days was I injured or killed because of defective tires.
NONE of these days did I have a wreck with my granddaughter in the car.

ALL of these days I had been the recipient of traveling mercies.
ALL of these days my tires were held up on the road by God's strong hands.
ALL of these days I was safe on earth through grace.

December 8, 2016 THIS day thanking God for his protection in dangers unawares.
THIS day feeling safe and relieved.
THIS day feeling blessed.

And Nothing Happened

The Lord protects those of childlike faith; I was facing death, and he saved me.

Psalm 116:6 NLT

Back in the winter, as Chad was leaving my house, he looked at my tires and said, "Mom, your tires are dry-rotted." I had only had them a short while. They still had 35,000 miles of tread left, and anyway, I don't drive much.

A couple months later, I read a consumer article that said if a person does not do a lot of driving, the tires will dry rot! So Chad was right. But I still could not see the fissures that would indicate dry rot.

In early summer, I began losing air, first in a back tire, next in a front tire. I soon became a pro at putting my 50 cents in the air machine and re-inflating my tires. In June, I took my car in for routine maintenance and asked my mechanic to look at the tires. "Them tires is pretty dry-rotted," was his diagnosis also. I believed him because he does not sell tires.

In July, the grandkids were coming. I was low on money, as well as air, but just to be safe, I made an appointment to get new tires. The first words out of the store owner's mouth were, "Ooh, they're dry-rotted. If you'd had a blowout with a dry-rotted tire, it would've been worse than a regular blow-out. It could have been fatal." Finally convinced, I pulled out my Discover card and paid for new tires.

Looking back, I realize God protected me every day I drove on those old tires, in spite of multiple warnings that I did not heed. What could have been a disaster never happened. I bowed my head and thanked Him for unknown averted catastrophes—for protections unawares—and for the days nothing happened.

Wired

The fruit of righteousness will be peace; the effect of righteousness will be quietness and confidence forever.

ISAIAH 32:17 NIV

Chris was at work, so I waited in his new studio apartment above a garage for the electric company to come and hook up his Internet. To get to Chris's place required a treacherous trudge up 20 steep stairs. The man arrived promptly at 10 a.m., as we had scheduled. He identified himself as Steve.

He was a calm, older man, who set about connecting cables and wires. For a second, he thought he had brought the wrong wire, which would have necessitated another tromp down and back up the stairs. Then he was relieved to find that he did indeed have the right one.

"That's a miracle," I half joked. He softly and seriously said, "It's a blessing." Here was a man who was a quiet witness, confident enough in his faith to recognize a true blessing, even as small as the right wire, and a save from navigating those steps again.

The Woman At The Bus Stop

A joyful heart is good medicine, but a crushed spirit dries up the bones.

PROVERBS 17:22 NIV

Yesterday, I was walking downtown by the bus stop. A frail young woman with a little girl asked me the time. She had forgotten her phone, and was afraid she would miss the bus. As she lovingly pulled the little girl's hair back in with a rubber band, she told me that her car had blown up this week, and that her boyfriend's car wasn't running. Her vocational rehabilitation counselor, though, had given her some bus vouchers. Those few sentences told me a lot.

She was a single mother with no job, no transportation, and no money to repair her car. Her boyfriend couldn't take care of himself, it seemed, much less her and her child. That she had a vocational rehab counselor told me she had a physical and/or mental disability that was preventing her from working, but that she was trying to improve her life.

Pity pierced my heart. What a forlorn situation, I thought. Then, with a cheerful smile, the woman looked up and said, "Well, at least I'm saving money on gas." She never asked me for a handout. In the midst of a hard life that would drive some of us to despair, she was able to see a flicker of brightness.

Would we feel the same in her situation? I wished her a blessed day, and lifted up a silent prayer for her. Then I was on my way, thanking God for my small problems and taking inspiration from the woman at the bus stop.

You Might Get What You Need

Don't worry about anything; instead, pray about everything. Tell God what you need, and thank Him for all he has done. Then you will experience God's peace, which exceeds anything we can understand. His peace will guard your hearts and minds as you live in Christ Jesus.

PHILIPPIANS 4:5-7 NIV

Yesterday I had two insurance bills due, and no way of paying them. I went to bed with a prayer of supplication in my heart and a gnawing ache of worry in my stomach. Yesterday my business account balance was $0.00.

Today I decided, for some unknown reason (probably desperation), to check it again. When the recording said my balance was $435.23, I was astounded! An unexpected case fee had been deposited overnight! The total due on my insurance bills was $432, leaving me with a balance of $3.23. That fee met my needs.

There was no room left for pleasure, except for the pleasure of relief, and a sweet iced tea. I went to my stack of music CDs, pulled out the Rolling Stones Greatest Hits, and listened as Mick Jagger belted out, "You don't always get what you want, but if you try real hard, you might get what you need." Oh, yes indeed!

Was Weak, But Now...

The Lord is righteous in all His ways and loving toward all he has made. The Lord is near to all who call on him, to all who call on him in truth. He fulfills the desires of those who fear him; he hears their cry and saves them.

Psalm 145:17-19 NIV

I have always been the strong one, the independent one, the one friends and family could count on for counsel and support. I, as we all have, have survived crises—the death of a spouse, health problems, clinical depressions, and betrayal. Stoically, not asking for help, or even acknowledging my own needs, I should have expected the fall. How foolish to live one's life without seeking the counsel and support of God.

That night, I was worried. There is no worry like that for your children. My boy was trying mightily and I was so proud of him, but he was sinking into a deep pool of debt—and there was no relief in sight. His debt had become mine because I love him, but often I did not have money for enough groceries, because I was buying them for his family. I, too, began to sink financially and emotionally.

I had done all I could. In my fear, I cried out to God through my tears, but He already knew that I was sick and weak with worry. He heard me, and He answered me. Oh, there was no unexpected giant windfall or a better job with better pay for my son; but within two days of my prayers, his financial burden (and thus mine) was lifted by a generous offer from his father of housing in exchange for some maintenance work.

In desperation, my son had admitted his problems to his father, as never before. In love and compassion, his father had answered. In desperation, I had reached out to my heavenly Father, and in love and compassion, He had responded. His miraculous ways are there for the asking. Ask Him now.

Happily Ever After

"For I know the plans I have for you," declares the Lord, "plans to prosper you and not to harm you, plans to give you hope and a future."

Jeremiah 29:11 NIV

She was devastated. She had given her body to a man, who proclaimed to love her. Now she was pregnant. Now the man she loved proclaimed he was not so sure about the love word. He reluctantly agreed to marry her.

She shopped hurriedly for a "shotgun" wedding dress. She tried it on to show me. She looked beautiful, but her tears betrayed her. That was the last time she wore that dress. She was the one who called off the wedding, because she knew in her heart the marriage would be disastrous.

She vowed to love and take care of her baby. And she did. She named him Jackson. She settled into single motherhood and a low-paying job. Her employer did let her bring Jackson to work with her the first year, so she didn't have to pay a babysitter.

Two years later, she was at a downtown music festival, where she ran into Jake, a guy she had known in high school. There on the street, Jake took a chance and proclaimed that he had loved her since she was 17. She was skeptical; she even gave him a hard time, but Jake stayed around. He pampered her. He loved Jackson too. He proposed by candlelight one night over pizza.

She shopped happily for the perfect wedding dress. She chose a beautiful, ivory, long mermaid gown with a sweetheart neckline and a teal sash. She tried it on to show me. She looked beautiful, and her tears were happy. She knew in her heart this marriage was right.

The wedding in the country church was spiritual. Jake was handsome in a black suit with a teal tie that matched her sash. Little Jackson looked dapper as he carried the rings down the aisle. Jake's niece smiled in pink chiffon as she too happily scattered rose petals onto the carpet.

She cried. Jake cried. I cried. Happy tears.

Now several years later, they love each other more. They own their house with two acres. They have a baby girl. Most wonderful is that Jake adopted Jackson. Now they are a real family. This is God's plan for her, not a life of hardship and poverty. This is her happily ever after.

The Whole World

They will be called oaks of righteousness, a planting of the Lord for the display of his splendor.

Isaiah 61:3 NIV

I live in a fishbowl of downtown activity, For privacy, I keep my top shutters open, and a curtain drawn across the bottom half of my living room window. I can see the seasons change in the tops of the trees—sparkling ice-covered winter branches, slowly coming alive with tiny neon buds in the spring, then bursting into the full-bodied green of summer. Today, the leaves were turning to early fall's pale orange and yellow. I enjoyed what I saw so much, I pulled back the curtain—and it changed my whole view!

Where I had only seen the tops, now the whole trees stood out, lit by a beacon of bright sunlight, so much clearer than the tops alone. Patches of happy blue sky punctuated the changing leaves. My spirit soared at the glorious sight I had been missing.

How many times do we see or live life half-full? Nothing is wrong; we might even be satisfied and content. But don't settle for less; half is good, but full is better. Once we open ourselves to the whole world and its possibilities for genuine beauty of the soul, all becomes right with the world.

Made in the USA
Columbia, SC
08 October 2018